A
Tolkien
Compass

A
Tolkien
Compass

Edited by
JARED LOBDELL

OPEN COURT
Chicago and La Salle, Illinois

To order books from Open Court, call toll free 1-800-815-2280, or visit our website at www.opencourtbooks.com.

Open Court Publishing Company is a division of Carus Publishing Company.

This book is a new edition of the work of the same title published in 1975 by Open Court. The first edition contained 'Guide to the Names in *The Lord of the Rings*', by J.R.R. Tolkien. Regrettably, the Tolkien Estate has objected strongly to its inclusion in any reprint of *A Tolkien Compass*, so it has been dropped from this new edition.

Second edition:
First printing 2003

Printed and bound in the United States of America

Library of Congress Cataloging-in-Publication Data

A Tolkien compass / edited by Jared Lobdell.
    p. cm.
   Includes bibliographical references and index.
   ISBN 0-87548-303-8 (alk. paper)
   1. Tolkien, J.R.R. (John Ronald Reuel), 1892–1973—Criticism and interpretation 2. Fantasy fiction, English—History and criticism. 3. Middle Earth (Imaginary place) I. Lobdell, Jared, 1937–
PR6039.O32 Z843 2002
823'.912—dc21

                         2002192495

Contents

Foreword by Tom Shippey   vii

Introduction   1

1.   Gollum's Character Transformation in *The Hobbit*
     BONNIEJEAN CHRISTENSEN   7

2.   The Psychological Journey of Bilbo Baggins
     DOROTHY MATTHEWS   27

3.   The Fairy-tale Morality of *The Lord of the Rings*
     WALTER SCHEPS   41

4.   The Corruption of Power
     AGNES PERKINS and HELEN HILL   55

5.   Everyclod and Everyhero: The Image of Man in Tolkien
     DEBORAH C. ROGERS   67

6.   The Interlace Structure of *The Lord of the Rings*
     RICHARD C. WEST   75

7.   Narrative Pattern in *The Fellowship of the Ring*
     DAVID M. MILLER   93

8.   'The Scouring of the Shire': Tolkien's View of Fascism
     ROBERT PLANK   105

9.   Hell and The City: Tolkien and the Traditions of
     Western Literature
     CHARLES A. HUTTAR   115

10.   Aspects of the Paradisiacal in Tolkien's Work
     U. MILO KAUFMANN   141

Postscript by Jared Lobdell   151

Index   159

Foreword

The ten critical essays which follow come from what one might call the Age of Innocence of Tolkien studies. Jared Lobdell, introducing them back in 1975, could survey the field in a single paragraph, his second, and could claim that *A Tolkien Compass* was the first occasion on which Tolkien 'fans' could see their work and their opinions collected. Things are very different now. If one wants to survey the field of Tolkien studies, it is necessary first to look at Richard C. West's *Tolkien: An Annotated Checklist, Revised Edition* (Kent, Ohio: Kent State University Press, 1981), second, at Judith A. Johnson's *J.R.R. Tolkien: Six Decades of Criticism* (Westport, Ct: Greenwood, 1986), and third, bringing matters up to the present day, at the long bibliography by Michael Drout, Hilary Wynne, and Melissa Higgins, 'Scholarly Studies of J.R.R. Tolkien and his Works (in English), 1984–2000' in *Envoi* vol. 9, no. 2 (Fall 2000), pp. 135–165. These three works between them contain several hundred pages of studies, with entries now running well into the thousands.

Tolkien studies have moreover not only become more frequent, they have become increasingly professionalized. It was unlikely, in 1975, that any professional critic could gain tenure at a recognized university by writing on Tolkien, while in the United Kingdom at least, professing an interest in Tolkien was almost certain death for any hopeful candidate seeking entrance to a department of English. Residual hostility to Tolkien remains strong in the critical profession and the media, showing itself in remarks such as Judith Shulevitz's in the *New York Times Book Review* as recently as 22nd April, 2001, that Tolkien's mission has turned out to be "death to literature itself," or in Germaine Greer's response to Tolkien's victory in a readers' poll organized by Waterstone's bookstores: "it has been my nightmare that Tolkien would turn out to be the most influential writer of the twentieth century. The bad dream has materialised" (*W Magazine*, Winter 1997). However, readers' polls in the end cannot be denied, certainly not when they keep coming up with the same answer, and certainly not in departments of English increasingly anxious to attract students alienated by much of what has been recommended to them. So taking up Tolkien studies is now, as it was not thirty years ago, a not unreasonable 'career move'.

It may be doubted whether this has much improved the level of criticism offered. One great advantage which the amateur possesses over the professional is candor: Amateurs write what they want to, not what they feel will be acceptable, or will fit an ideology. And criticism from the Age of Innocence possesses a quality of surprise, perhaps of having been surprised, which can no longer be counterfeited. The studies which follow start many trains of thought which have in the end become accepted wisdom, but to their authors they were new, and this can still be felt. At the same time there are some ideas which have lost their luster, some statements of fact which have since been disproved. As one who began writing on Tolkien in the same year that the *Tolkien Compass* came out, only to find many confident assertions flattened by the appearance of *The Silmarillion*, the *Unfinished Tales*, the twelve volumes of 'The History of Middle-earth', and several volumes of criticism and of children's writing, I can only sympathize with those disproved. Nevertheless it is good for critics to predict, and good for their predictions to be put to the test. Without disproof there can be no advance, and there can be no disproof where nothing has been asserted. For all these reasons—freshness, candor, and a sense of historical depth—one should welcome the reprinting of *A Tolkien Compass*, while at the same time deploring the required omission from it of Tolkien's own immensely valuable 'Guide to the Names in *The Lord of the Rings*'.

Turning to look at the ten essays singly and separately, one can indeed see that some of their guesses were right and some wrong. Robert Plank remarks (though it is a view he is actually concerned to deny) that "*The Lord of the Rings* was conceived in its totality, and to a great extent written, prior to World War II." Whoever said that, it was not correct. We now know that Tolkien started work on *The Lord of the Rings* in December 1937, and when war broke out 21 months later he had still not got very far; see *The Return of the Shadow*, edited by Christopher Tolkien (Houghton Mifflin, 1988). Charles Huttar likewise quotes John Donne, and says that his words "have puzzled source hunters, for they do not directly follow known legends." They would not have puzzled Tolkien—much though he probably disliked Donne as a Catholic apostate—for Tolkien was well aware of a really old English Christian tradition, in which not only did Calvary stand on the same spot as the Garden of Eden, but the Annunciation, the Crucifixion, and the Fall of Man took place on the same day, March 25th, not at all coincidentally the day of the destruction of the Ring: See, for instance, the reference given in my *The Road to Middle-earth* (Houghton Mifflin, revised edn., 2003), in note 16 to chapter 6. Tolkien has, in short, been placed much more securely in the context of his own time, and also in the longer context of literary and theological history. Much more is now known about his life, and about his literary and personal relationships (especially with C.S. Lewis and the other members of 'the Inklings', or as they are now often called, 'the Oxford Christians'.)

Some things, then, have moved on. Others have become firmly established. Bonniejean Christensen's article on the changes between editions of *The Hobbit* is exactly on the mark, and though one can follow the changes now more readily in Wayne Hammond and Douglas Anderson's magisterial *J.R.R. Tolkien: A Descriptive Bibliography* (Oak Knoll Books, 1993), and in Douglas Anderson's *Annotated Hobbit* (revised edn., Houghton Mifflin, 2002), her conclusions remain undeniable. Few would argue with Agnes Perkins and Helen Hill, either, about 'The Corruption of Power' as *the* theme of *The Lord of the Rings*, though one might wonder whether it is desire for power that corrupts, or the actual experience of having it. I cannot agree with Deborah Rogers about Aragorn as "the Image of Man," though she does stimulate an interesting argument. Everyone has their own favorite characters in *The Lord of the Rings*—mine is Uglúk the orc, a man or rather a monster who knows the value of discipline—but favorites aside, it is Frodo who is the 'type' of Christ, though in saying this a non-typological age should remember that all types of Christ must fail and be inadequate, till the true Redeemer comes. I cannot agree either with Robert Plank about fascism as Tolkien's target in "The Scouring of the Shire." It seems to me that, just as in George Orwell's *Nineteen Eighty-Four*, published five years before *The Fellowship of the Ring*, the main similarity is neither with Italian Fascism nor with Russian Communism, but with

'Ingsoc', or English Socialism, a seedy, second-rate, and com-
mendably half-hearted version of the great Continental despo-
tisms. The parallels with Orwell, and with William Golding's
Lord of the Flies, a work which came out in the same year as *The
Fellowship of the Ring*, indeed deserve to be drawn out further:
In Golding's work, too, what ought to be an idyllic existence for
a band of English choirboys stranded in what could easily
become a tropical version of the Shire turns instead into something reminiscent of Uglúk, or Gríshnakh, even more than of
Saruman.

Three areas touched on in this volume meanwhile seem to
me to be still highly productive, each of them represented by
two essays. I am no believer in Jungian analyses, but Dorothy
Matthews's 'The Psychological Journey of Bilbo Baggins' does
seem to me to have got something, which calls out to be
extended to the greater structure of *The Lord of the Rings*. It may
have something to do with the structure, if not exactly the
morality, of fairy-tale, as considered by Walter Scheps. Fairy-
tales do seem—think of 'Cinderella', or 'Beauty and the Beast',
or 'Rapunzel'—to be in some way about growing up, though
they can also be about *refusing* to grow up. Think here of J.M.
Barrie's *Peter Pan*, or even 'Jack and the Beanstalk', where Jack
cuts down the beanstalk (a phallic symbol?), kills the giant (a
father-figure?), and goes home to live with his Mom (surely a
symbol of something or other). Tolkien's work has often been
accused of lacking full adult status. I do not think this is true at
all, but I think he, and the unknown authors of fairy-tale, often
have better intuitions about how adulthood is to be achieved
than one finds in self-help books and the works of literary critics. The last pages of *The Lord of the Rings*, with the hero slowly
withering, or fading, and eventually being taken away not to
immortality but in search of an uncertain cure, reject all conventional versions of the conventional happy ending. Sam's
"Well, I'm back" says all that many people have been able to say
after an irretrievable loss.

Another essay which has been proven exactly right is Richard
West's essay on 'interlace'—only Tolkien is more interlaced than
that! I do not think anyone has yet plumbed the full intricacies
of Tolkien's deliberate cross-referencing from one area of plot to
another, indicated by careful remarks about dates, times, and the
phases of the moon, but West's work is a good place to start.

The sense of cycles and spirals is also marked, as David Miller here points out. One might wonder, reading the volumes of 'The History of Middle-earth', whether these were not created in part by Tolkien's work habits, rewriting continually, but doing so in what Christopher Tolkien calls "phases," or surges, each one rolling a little further up the beach.

Finally, and appropriately, one comes to Heaven and Hell, or rather Paradise and Hell, as discussed here by U. Milo Kaufmann and Charles Huttar. Hell for Tolkien, that tree-hugger *par excellence*, the hater of chainsaws and motor traffic, is the city. And Paradise? Paradise is not the same as Heaven, because—as is pointed out in a work Tolkien knew well, the medieval classic *Mandeville's Travels*—once upon a time it was on Earth, and perhaps one day it will be again. For Tolkien, it may have been the pool by Sarehole Mill, where he spent the happiest years of his childhood, and which he lamented as completely destroyed, taken over by the city sprawl, when he visited it many years later (see Humphrey Carpenter's *Biography*, Houghton Mifflin 1977, pp. 124–25).

The pool is actually still there, indeed within the urban sprawl of Birmingham, England's major manufacturing city, and as pointed out by David Bratman in *Mallorn* for December 1999, p. 7, moved by bureaucrats from Tolkien's beloved Worcestershire to the neighboring county of Warwickshire. Yet it remains to my eye surprisingly unaffected. When I last visited it, moving quietly through its screen of bushes, there was a large and splendid blue heron standing motionless in the water. It was so motionless that I eventually said to my old friend Paul (like me and Professor Tolkien, a former player for the Old Edwardians Rugby Football Club), "it's not real, it's a dummy one someone's put there." At this the heron spread its wings and flew majestically away. Tolkien would have been pleased, I am sure, to see authoritative opinion so clearly refuted by brute fact, and even more pleased to see the heron in the pool. Almost a hundred years after he left Sarehole for good, beauty is coming back. And thirty years after his death, interest in his vision of beauty has never been higher. As its title suggests, *A Tolkien Compass* provides in the search for this an essential orientation.

TOM SHIPPEY
Saint Louis University

Introduction

The papers printed here have rather a curious history. Eight of them (four at each) were presented at the First and Second Conferences on Middle Earth, organized by Jan Finder, and held, respectively, in Urbana, Illinois, in 1969, and in Cleveland, Ohio, in 1971. He gave these papers, and a number of others presented at those conferences, to Mr. Richard West, the compiler of *Tolkien Criticism: An Annotated Checklist* and Editor of the occasional journal *Orcrist*. At my suggestion, Mr. West chose those papers that he believed merited publication and turned them over to me to prepare for the press. By eliminating those from his selection that did not bear directly on Tolkien, and by limiting all contributors to a single contribution, I came up with eight of the ten papers included in this book. The other two papers were prepared for the planned Third Conference on Middle Earth in Pleasantville, New York, in 1973, that was never held.

As of the publication of this book, there have already been two volumes of critical essays devoted to Tolkien—*Mankato Studies in English*, Volume 2, No. 1 (Mankato, Mn, 1967), and Neil Isaacs and Rose Zimbardo, eds., *Tolkien and the Critics* (Notre Dame, 1968)—in addition to five book-length studies. Articles on Tolkien can be found in several periodicals; there is *Orcrist*, which is among other things, the Bulletin of the Modern Language Association Seminar on Medieval Tradition in the Modern Arts. Another important journal is *Mythlore*, which has incorporated the *Tolkien Journal* and includes articles on other writers as well. *Mythlore* is the journal of the Mythopoeic Society, which has also published (in mimeographed form) the proceedings of their conferences, including material on Tolkien. And, too, there is an unusual book by Gracia Fay Ellwood, *Good News from Middle Earth* (Grand Rapids, 1970), which discusses Tolkien with some illumination. In the face of all this, I suspect it may be asked, is this book necessary? Why publish the proceedings of still more conferences?

Of course, it can be argued that Tolkien is a major writer whose work is especially open to serious misrepresentation, both on the 'Oo! Those Awful Orcs' level of Edmund Wilson and by those who read and revere *The Lord of the Rings*, but it is not the real reason for this book. Indeed, one or two of the papers published here seem to me (though not, of course, to their authors) to show signs of misinterpretation, even though they are well written, lucidly argued, and stimulating—in the case of those I disagree with, infuriatingly so.

More to the point, criticism of Tolkien has tended, under-standably, to shy away from the basic question 'What is it all about?' There are, of course, notable exceptions—I can think of reviews by Auden, Lewis, Edmund Fuller, and several others—but it seems to me that in general those who have written about Tolkien have been too concerned with attacking or defending him, or else too concerned about the Tolkien craze to do his work justice. It is my contention that this book sticks closely to Tolkien's text (though in differing degrees in the different papers) and that in this lies one essential justification for its being published. Not, of course, that I agree with everything said in the different papers: as I have already made clear, I do not. But if some of the authors misread Tolkien, at least it is quite clearly Tolkien they are misreading.

Finally, this book represents the first time that the Tolkien 'fans' have had a chance to have their work collected for com-mercial publication. The *Mankato Studies* were in fact the pro-ceedings of a conference, but they have not made the bookshelves of local stores. *Tolkien and the Critics* included some previously published works, but only one 'fan' magazine article, and that one in truncated form. Yet there is a body of scholars who are Tolkien fans, who attend the various confer-ences, who have published in the *Tolkien Journal, Mythlore,* and *Orcrist)* receiving no scholarly credit for their efforts (except for *Orcrist*). This book is, in a way, their showcase. It is designed to show that within the world of Tolkien fans there is scholarship, high seriousness, and good writing. I believe it does show precisely that.

In what follows in this introduction, I have taken the liberty not only of mentioning points made in the chapters but also of disagreeing with a few of them. Probably this is not the proper function of an editor, but the disagreement will suffice to show (if nothing else) that those who agree on Tolkien's status do not always agree on what he means—and, what is much more important to me, I think I owe it to Professor Tolkien to protest what I consider to be wrongheaded interpretations although it may, in the end, turn out that I am the one who is wrongheaded. At the same time, I owe it to the authors whose work I am editing to print what they wrote despite my disagreements.

Two of the chapters discuss *The Hobbit*. Bonniejean Christensen of the University of North Dakota gives an illuminating account of the changes in the text of Chapter V of *The Hobbit* between the 1937 and 1951 (and 1966) editions. I am profoundly unsympathetic to Dorothy Matthews's approach in her discussion of 'The Psychological Journey of Bilbo Baggins', but I believe she carries it off well. The reasons I find myself unsympathetic to this approach have been adequately summarized by the late C.S. Lewis in his essay on 'Psychoanalysis and Literary Criticism'. In that essay, he explains that "a story about a golden dragon plucking the apple of immortality in a garden at the world's end, and a dream about one's pen going through the paper while one scribbles a note, are, in Freudian terms the same story," although they are entirely different as literature. Just so. Yet, as he also wrote in that same essay, "psychoanalysis heals some of the wounds made by materialism," and if "the general effect of materialism is to give you . . . a flat wall only a few inches away," then "psychoanalysis offers you some kind of depth back again" (Lewis, *Selected Literary Essays*, pp. 296, 299). And that is my justification for including Professor Matthews's study.

The next four chapters deal generally with *The Lord of the Rings*. Walter Scheps of the Ohio State University presents a well-written (and by my view wrongheaded) discussion of 'The Fairy-tale Morality of *The Lord of the Rings*', a paper which calls to my mind the equally wrongheaded article by Mr. Matthews Hodgart in the *New York Review of Books* some years ago, in which he complained that "for a parallel in medieval literature we must look to works written under the inspiration of Christian doctrine: to the *Chanson de Roland*, with its straight conflict between good Christians and bad Saracens." Evidently, this is a continuing complaint against Professor Tolkien—whether, as in Mr. Hodgart's case, it is couched as an attack on moral absolutism, or as in Professor Scheps's article, it is (at least in part) directed at the presumed irrelevance of moral absolutism. Granted that one can—and many do—push the demand for relevance too far and that to try to sell us on the principle that the black-and-white morality of *The Lord of the Rings* cannot be applied *volens-nolens* to real life is not to try to sell us on moral relativism, this is still merchandise that I am not buying. Yet it is well sold: Professor Scheps argues the point cogently. Perhaps the article's publication here will lead someone to write as cogent an answer.

Agnes Perkins and Helen Hill of Eastern Michigan University, and Deborah Rogers, find little fault in Tolkien's 'paiens ont tort et chrestiens ont droit'—or, to be more exact, his 'good and evil have not changed, nor are they one thing for elves and another for men and hobbits'. In fact they rejoice in finding in *The Lord of the Rings* the marks of consistent Catholic doctrine. As their title, 'The Corruption of Power', suggests, Professor Perkins and Hill argue that *The Lord of the Rings* illustrates Lord Acton's dictum, though the lesson implicit in "all power tends to corrupt" was given a more memorable form nineteen centuries before Acton—"lay not up for yourself treasures upon earth." And Mrs. Rogers, noting that "individually we are hobbits; collectively we are Aragorn," has hit upon a precise temporal parallel to the belief that in our essential nature, individually we are men, collectively we are the body of Christ. I suspect it is needless to say that I agree with both papers, and very strongly indeed with Mrs. Rogers (except, to be sure, in her view that prospective members of any Tolkien Society should be told that the books "are about people who like beer and don't want to get in adventures").

Mr. Richard West discusses Tolkien's general narrative technique, the technique for which French critics invented the word *entrelacement* and which C.S. Lewis called "polyphonic narrative." Since I requested Mr. West to prepare a revised version of this paper for the Third Conference on Middle Earth—it dates in an earlier form from the first issue of *Orcrist*—it may reasonably (and correctly) be inferred that I think it a valuable piece of work. It should be pointed out that what Mr. West is doing is not a study of Tolkien's narrative pattern, but a study of the technique according to which Tolkien sets up the pattern: his paper serves to introduce, not contradict, Professor Miller's essay.

The next two chapters concern portions—large or small—of *The Lord of the Rings*. David Miller of Purdue is a contributor both to the *Mankato Studies in English* volume on Tolkien and to *Orcrist*. In 'The Narrative Pattern of *The Fellowship of the Ring*' he analyzes the formal relationship between the map and the structure of the two books which make up *The Fellowship*. The latter point is welcome not only because it is critical, but also (and to me especially) because Professor Miller is taking account of the author's division of the entire work into six books, not three.

Dr. Robert Plank, of the Department of Psychology at Case Western Reserve University, has taken a close look at 'The Scouring of the Shire', with rather interesting results. For one thing, he remarks (quite correctly) that, except for the dissolution of Saruman's body and, of course, the prevalence of hobbits, the episode is purely realistic in our terms as well as those of Tolkien's secondary universe. For another, he argues that the lesson of 'The Scouring' is not only transcendent and moral but quotidian and political as well. And, finally, he suggests that Saruman's—Sharkey's—government of the Shire is precisely fascism in action. Here, I confess, I begin to edge away from him. I fear that 'fascism' is not a useful term (considering how it has been bandied about in recent years, it is possibly misleading): I would not have used it. But the system of overgovernment that Dr. Plank describes, whatever it may be called, is unquestionably a menace in our world as it is in the Shire. Yet for them, as he points out, things are easier: they have a king reigning in Gondor. (Those who agree with me about the personal heresy in literary criticism may be put off by Dr. Plank's opening paragraph, but I think they will enjoy much of what follows.)

Professor Charles Huttar, of Hope College, beginning with Donne's "We think that Paradise and Calvarie/Christs Crosse, and Adams tree, stood in one place," follows two images—one might say myths—down through Western literature and into Tolkien's creation. The essay seems to me particularly valuable in its reminder that the myths, images, archetypes of which Tolkien makes use are not merely decorative. They have a significance— a *significatio* if you like—and what they signify is not one thing for *Beowulf* or the *Eddas* or *Gawain* or *The Faerie Queene*, and another for *The Lord of the Rings*. In this way at least (I think in others also), Tolkien's work, if *sui generis* in our time, is part of the old Western tradition which still reaches us across the chasm of the Industrial Revolution. (I confess that Freudian interpretations of the images make me skeptical, but they are mercifully brief in Professor Huttar's essay.)

Finally, Milo Kaufmann, of the University of Illinois, discusses Tolkien's conception of Paradise (by which Professor Kaufmann means a "sublime finitude") as it appears in 'Leaf by Niggle'. In Professor Kaufmann's view, Bombadil is precisely a creature of Paradise (here he is echoed by Mrs. Rogers, among others), and Paradise—in the world of *The Lord of the Rings*—is not enough. One needs to go beyond the circles of the world.

No one, in these chapters, is playing the game of *Quellenforschung*, which may be a good thing. But I should like to see someone (perhaps I will do it myself) attack the question of whose writing has influenced Professor Tolkien. Once he gets beyond one or two authors (Rider Haggard and G.K. Chesterton perhaps), I cry him caution: nonetheless, I should like to see it properly done, perhaps at a future conference on Middle Earth, if there is one. I hope these chapters suggest that there should be.

I shall not follow Mr. William Ready's example and dedicate this book to Professor Tolkien. (I will not, in fact, follow Mr. Ready's example in any way, shape, or form that I can avoid.) I will dedicate it rather—with, I trust, the permission of those whose papers it contains—to the followers of Tolkien, wherever, and in whatever guise.

Jared C. Lobdell
Ridgefield, Connecticut
September 1974

1

Gollum's Character Transformation in *The Hobbit*

BONNIEJEAN CHRISTENSEN

J.R.R. Tolkien's fallen hobbit, Gollum, is an interesting character in his own right, but the changes in his character that Tolkien made between the first edition of *The Hobbit* [1] in the 1930s and second edition in the 1950s make him one of his most fascinating creations. These alterations clearly grew from the demands of *The Lord of the Rings* [2] and reflect Tolkien's growing awareness of the dramatic possibilities of transforming a 'run-of-the-forge' ring into a sentient and malevolent source of evil. As I have shown elsewhere [3] Tolkien remade Gollum's role and character in the mold of Grendel and his dam and Unferth to fit his larger conception of the cosmic struggle between good and evil.

The Hobbit examines the nature of evil and the limits of man's response to it, a fact often overlooked because the tone of *The Hobbit* identifies it as a fantasy belonging in the nursery. In general Tolkien carefully avoided this tone [4] in *The Lord of the Rings,* which examines the same problems with different points of reference. *The Hobbit* examines evil through a series of encounters with monsters in increasing significance—the same pattern as in *Beowulf*—while *The Lord of the Rings* examines evil in metaphors that are both more pervasive—the eye of Sauron—and more abstract—the ringwraiths. As a consequence, Gollum's function differs in the two works. In *The Hobbit* he is one of a series of fallen creatures on a rising scale of terror. In *The Lord of the Rings* he is an example of the damned individual who loses his own soul because of devotion to evil (symbolized by the ring) but who, through grace, saves others. Critics have ignored the way grace operates through Gollum in *The Lord of the Rings,* but I do not think that definitive statements can be made about the nature of the work and Tolkien's intentions until it is explored more fully. I will examine the transformation in Gollum's character, the enlargement of his role and the changed nature of the ring between the first and second editions of *The Hobbit* as a means of emphasizing the importance Tolkien attaches to Gollum and of encouraging others to consider more seriously the role of Gollum in *The Lord of the Rings.*

'Riddles in the Dark', the fifth chapter of *The Hobbit,* is critical. In the first edition, Gollum is a lost soul who would kill but who would not violate his oath; he freely offers a ring as a prize to Bilbo in a riddle contest and when he loses and is unable to produce the ring, courteously shows Bilbo the way out of the mountain. In the second hardback edition, published before *The Lord of the Rings* appeared in Britain but after it appeared in the United States, Gollum is a withered, totally depraved creature dominated by an evil Ring and capable of any crime. In the Ballantine paperback edition of 1965 there are no further changes, but in the 1966 revision there are some very minor changes to give emphasis to Gollum's depravity and to eliminate references that still showed where the two versions were stitched together.

Gollum's Depravity

The great difference in the first and second hardback edition is in the second half of the chapter. The first half is unchanged, but the second is doubled in length. The revision increases the complexity of the chapter, beginning with the substitution of one prize for another in the riddle contest, going on to the change in Gollum's character and the transformation of the ring into a malevolent and sentient being, then developing the concept of Bilbo as a thief and concluding with the terrifying escape through the tunnels.

In the citations that follow, the original version is on the left and the revision is on the right unless otherwise noted. The page numbers for the left column refer to the Allen and Unwin edition of 1937 and the Houghton Mifflin edition of 1938. The two sets of page numbers for the right column refer to the hard-back editions of 1954 and 1958 and to the Ballantine editions of 1965 and 1966.

The first change in Chapter 5 involves the prize—the substitution of help in finding a way out of the mountain for the original present of a ring. This change is slight, involving just a few words, but it redirects the whole chapter. Gollum suggests a riddle contest, with Bilbo to become a meal if he cannot answer the riddles, and with Gollum to provide a prize if he can:

"If it asks us, and we doesn't answer, we gives it a present, gollum!" (p. 85).	"If it asks us, and we doesn't answer, then we does what it wants, eh? We shows it the way out, yes!" (p. 85, p. 81).

In this exchange Gollum refers to himself and to Bilbo as "precious." In the revised edition the word of endearment is extended to the Ring, which in *The Lord of the Rings* becomes for Gollum the Pearl of Great Price, well worth his soul.

One minor revision was made to alter a previously uncorrected passage, showing that the original wager had involved a gift. "Bilbo was beginning to wonder what Gollum's present would be like" was neatly changed to "Bilbo was beginning to hope that the wretch would not be able to answer" (p. 82). The only other reference to "present" is simply changed to "guess":

"Well," said Bilbo, after giving him a long chance, "what about your present?" (p. 87).	"Well," said Bilbo, after giving him a long chance, "what about your guess?" (p. 87, p. 83).

The remainder of the riddle contest is unchanged, with Bilbo feeling more uncomfortable as it progresses and with the hungry Gollum appearing the likely winner.

Another minor, but important, revision aligns the introductory description of Gollum with his development in *The Lord of the Rings*. This change is accomplished by the addition of modifiers, which are indicated here by italics:

Deep down here by the dark water lived old Gollum, *a small slimy creature*. I don't know where he came from, nor who or what he was. He was Gollum—as dark as darkness, except for two big round pale eyes *in his thin face.* He had a *little* boat . . . (p. 79)

Then the extensive revisions begin.

Musing aloud, Bilbo asks himself, "What have I got in my pocket?" Gollum thinks this is a riddle and the desperate Bilbo does not correct him, but allows him three guesses. When Gollum is unable to answer the impossible question—a common Northern motif [5]—Bilbo becomes fearful and holds out his little sword. The revision of the passage significantly changes the character of Gollum.

But funnily enough he need not have been alarmed. For one thing Gollum had learned long ago was never, never to cheat at the riddle-game, which is a sacred one and of immense antiquity.	He knew, of course, that the riddle-game was sacred and of immense antiquity, and even wicked creatures were afraid to cheat when they played at it. But he felt he could not trust this slimy thing to keep any promise at a pinch. Any excuse would do for him to slide out of it. And after all that last question had not been a genuine riddle according to the ancient laws.
Also there was the sword. He simply sat and whispered (p. 91).	But at any rate Gollum did not at once attack him. He could see the sword in Bilbo's hand. He sat still, shivering and whispering. At last Bilbo could wait no longer (p. 91, p. 86).

In the original version Gollum may be a benighted creature, condemned to separation from his kind, but he is not totally depraved. The two most heinous crimes to Old Norse morality were murder and oath-breaking. Gollum may be guilty of the former but not of the latter, but in the revised version Gollum is not to be trusted at all and much is made of the fact that the question was not a "genuine" riddle, the implication being that Gollum could not be trusted to keep his word. Bilbo's reliance on his sword reinforces this suspicion in the revised version: in the earlier version the reference to the sword provides an anti-climactic tone; in the later version the sword is made into a menacing weapon, ensuring that "Gollum did not at once attack him."

In his expanded role Gollum's transformation, as seen in the following passage, is essential to an appreciation of *The Lord of the Rings.*

"What about the present?' asked Bilbo, not that he cared very much, still he felt that he had won it, pretty fairly, and in very difficult circumstances too.

"Must we give it the thing, preciouss? Yess, we must! We must fetch it, preciouss, and give it the present we promised."

So Gollum paddled back to his boat, and Bilbo thought he had heard the last of him. But he had not (p. 91).

"Well?" he said. "What about your promise? I want to go. You must show me the way."

"Did we say so, precious? Show the nasty little Baggins the way out, yes, yes. But what has it got in its pocketses, eh? Not string, precious, but not nothing. Oh no! gollum!"

"Never you mind," said Bilbo. "A promise is a promise."

"Cross it is, impatient, precious," hissed Gollum. "But it must wait, yes it must. We can't go up the tunnels so hasty. We must go and get some things first, yes, things to help us."

"Well, hurry up!" said Bilbo, relieved to think he was just making an excuse and did not mean to come back. What was Gollum talking about? What useful thing could he keep out on the dark lake? But he was wrong. Gollum did mean to come back. He was angry now and hungry. And he was a miserable wicked creature, and already he had a plan (pp. 91–92, p. 87).

The Ring Changes

In the original version, Gollum goes for the ring to give it to Bilbo. There is no indication of treachery. In the revised edition, Gollum is an unpleasant antagonist who calls names and is quite willing to cheat. The expanded revision creates interest in Gollum's possession on the island—the Ring—by having Bilbo ask himself questions about the "thing."

The following passage in the revision introduces the Ring, which, in *The Lord of the Rings*, we learn Gollum had acquired on his birthday by strangling a companion who had found it:

The hobbit was jut thinking of going back up the passage—having had quite enough of Gollum and the dark water's edge—when he heard him wailing and squeaking away in the gloom. He was on his island (of which, of course, Bilbo knew nothing), scrabbling here and there, searching and seeking in vain, and turning out his pockets.	Not far away was his island, of which Bilbo knew nothing, and there in his hiding-place he kept a few wretched oddments, and one very beautiful thing, very beautiful, very wonderful. He had a ring, a golden ring, a precious ring.
"Where iss it? Where iss it?" Bilbo heard his squeaking. "Lost, lost, my preciouss, lost, lost! Bless us and splash us! We haven't the present we promised, and we haven't even got it for ourselveses" (pp. 91–92).	"My birthday-present!" he whispered to himself, as he had often done in the endless dark days. "That's what we wants now, yes; we wants it!" (p. 92, p. 87).

The revision describes it as a Ring of Power; in the original it was only the regulation sort of magic ring. The passage from the original is transposed in the revision to indicate its properties to the reader before Bilbo is aware of them. The transposed passage is given here in italics:

for if you slipped that ring on your finger, you were invisible; only in the sunlight could you be seen, and then only by your shadow, and that was a faint and shaky sort of shadow (p. 92).	He wanted it because it was a ring of power, and if you slipped that ring on your finger, you were invisible; only in the full sunlight could you be seen, and then only by your shadow, and that would be shaky and faint (p. 92, p. 87).

The Master of Evil

In the original version the ring as birthday present is introduced here but without the sinister overtones of the revision, which make the Ring sentient and evil. The revision also introduces the Master, the force in opposition to good, known elsewhere as Sauron:

Bilbo turned round and waited, wondering what it could be that the creature was making such a fuss about. This proved very fortunate afterwards. For Gollum came back and made a tremendous spluttering and whispering and croaking; and in the end Bilbo gathered that Gollum had had a ring—a wonderful, beautiful ring, a ring that he had been given for a birthday present, ages and ages before in old days when such rings were less uncommon.	
	"My birthday-present! It came to me on my birthday, my precious! So he had always said to himself. But who knows how Gollum came by that present, ages ago in the old days when such rings were still at large in the world? Perhaps even the Master who ruled them could not have said. Gollum used to
Sometimes he had it in his pocket; usually he kept it in a	

little hole in the rock on his island; sometimes he wore it—

when he was very, very hungry, and tired of fish, and crept along dark passages looking for stray goblins. Then he might venture even into places where the torches were lit and made his eyes blink and smart; hut he would he safe. O yes! very nearly safe; for if you slipped that ring on your finger . . . (p. 92).

wear it at first, till it tired him; and then he kept it in a pouch next to his skin, till it galled him; and now usually he hid it in a hole in the rock on his island, and was always going back along dark passages to look at it. And still sometimes he put it on, when he could not bear to be parted from it any longer, or when he was very, very, hungry, and tired of fish. Then he would creep along dark passages looking for stray goblins. He might even venture into places where the torches were lit and made his eyes blink and smart; for he would he safe. Oh yes, quite safe. No one would see him . . . (p. 92, pp. 87–88).

The revision is expanded by a dozen lines dealing with Gollum's most recent meal, "a small goblin-imp," and his meditation on returning, invisible, and consuming Bilbo. The expanded revision then returns to material in the original and applies it, transposed in position and altered in meaning and tone:

The hobbit was just thinking of going back up the passage—having had quite enough of Gollum and the dark water's edge—when he heard him wailing and squeaking away in the gloom. He was on his island (of which, of course, Bilbo knew nothing), scrabbling here and there, searching and seeking in vain, and turning out his pockets.

Bilbo thought he had heard the last of him. Still he waited a while; for he had no idea how to find his way out alone.

Suddenly he heard a screech. It sent a shiver down his back. Gollum was cursing and wailing away in the gloom, not very far off by the sound of it. He was on his island, scrabbling here and

"Where iss it? Where iss it?" Bilbo heard him squeaking. Lost, lost, my preciouss, lost, lost! Bless us and splash us! We haven't the present we promised, and we haven't even got it for ourselves" (pp. 91–92).	there, searching and seeking in vain. "Where is it? Where iss it?" Bilbo heard him crying. "Losst it is, my precious, lost, lost! Curse us and crush us, my precious is lost!" (p. 93, p. 88).

In the revision, Bilbo's situation is seen as more desperate, for he realizes he does not know how to get out and he is menaced by a Gollum who screeches, curses, and wails at the loss of the Ring which would have enabled him to kill Bilbo. This is a different creature entirely from the opponent who squeaks his oaths—which consist of "Bless us and splash us!"—and laments for a loss that prevents his paying a wager. The revisions of Gollum's diction indicate the change in his character and anticipate the altered response he will have to the loss of the Ring in the later edition.

In the original version, Gollum is all apologies for being unable to keep his word. He is even willing to substitute an alternate prize. Bilbo realizes that the ring in his pocket must be Gollum's but, using an old saw as justification, decides to keep it and asks Gollum to get him out of the mountain. In the revision, Gollum does not disclose what he has lost and Bilbo has an understandably rough and unsympathetic attitude toward a character portrayed as sinister and threatening.

I don't know how many times Gollum begged Bilbo's pardon. He kept on saying: "We are ssorry; we didn't mean to cheat, we meant to give it our only present, if it won the competition." He even offered to catch Bilbo some nice juicy fish to eat as consolation.	"What's the matter?" Bilbo called. "What have you lost?" "It mustn't ask us," shrieked Gollum. "Not its business, no, gollum! It's losst, gollum, gollum, gollum!"

Bilbo shuddered at the thought of it. "No thank you!" he said as politely as he could.

He was thinking hard, and the idea came to him that Gollum must have dropped that ring sometime and that he must have found it, and that he had that very ring in his pocket. But he had the wits not to tell Gollum.

"Finding's keeping!" he said to himself; and being in a very tight place, I daresay, he was right. Anyway the ring belonged to him now.

"Never mind!" he said. "The ring would have been mine now, if you had found it; so you would have lost it anyway. And I will let you off on on condition."

"Yes, what iss it? What does it wish us to do, my precious?"

"Help me to get out of these places," said Bilbo (pp. 92–93).

"Well, so am I," cried Bilbo, "and I want to get unlost. And I won the game, and you promised. So come along! Come and let me out, and then go on with your looking!"

Utterly miserable as Gollum sounded, Bilbo could not find much pity in his heart, and he had a feeling that anything Gollum wanted so much could hardly he something good. "Come along" he shouted (p. 93, p. 88).

The Addictive Ring

In the revision almost a page of additional dialogue between Bilbo and Gollum follows, in which Bilbo attempts to discover what Gollum has lost while Gollum becomes increasingly suspicious of what Bilbo has in his pocket. Then both versions deal with Gollum's plans for Bilbo and then with Bilbo's exit from the mountain. The parallel material is, predictably, dissimilar. In the original version Gollum is true to the Norse ideal of keeping an oath, albeit with some difficulty. In the revision he is so enslaved to the Ring that nothing else matters, and he attempts to attack Bilbo.

Now Gollum had to agree to this, if he was not to cheat. He still very much wanted just to try what the stranger tasted like, but now he had to give up all idea of it. Still there was the little sword; and the stranger was wide awake and on the look out, not unsuspecting as Gollum liked to have the things which he attacked. So perhaps it was best after all.	But now the light in Gollum's eyes had become a green fire, and it was coming swiftly nearer. Gollum was in his boat again, paddling wildly back to the dark shore; and such a rage of loss and suspicion was in his heart that no sword had any more terror for him.
That is how Bilbo got to know that the tunnel ended at the water and went no further on the other side where the mountain wall was dark and solid. He also learned that he ought to have turned down one of the side passages to the right before he came to the bottom; but he could not follow Gollum's directions for finding it again on the way up, and he made the wretched creature come and show him the way (p. 93).	Bilbo could not guess what had maddened the wretched creature, but he saw that all was up, and that Gollum meant to murder him at any rate. Just in time he turned and ran blindly up the dark passage down which he had come, keeping close to the wall and feeling it with his left hand (p. 94, p. 89).

In the original version Bilbo, almost as a prank, slips on the ring to determine if Gollum's mumblings about it are accurate. In the revision the Ring is the actor of its own volition, and Bilbo is unaware of its magic properties.

	"What has it got in its pocketses?" he heard the hiss

As they went along up the tunnel together, Gollum flip-flapping at his side, Bilbo going very softly, he thought he would try the ring. He slipped it on his finger.

"Where iss it? Where iss it gone to?" said Gollum at once, peering about with his long eyes.

"Here I am, following behind!" said Bilbo slipping off the ring again, and feeling very pleased to have it and to find that it really did what Gollum said (p. 93).

loud behind him, and the splash as Gollum leapt from his boat. "What have I, I wonder?" he said to himself, as he panted and stumbled along. He put his left hand in his pocket. The ring felt very cold as it quietly slipped on to his groping forefinger.

The hiss was close behind him. He turned now and saw Gollum's eyes like small green lamps coming up the slope. Terrified he tried to run faster, but suddenly he struck his toes on a snag in the floor, and fell flat with his little sword under him (pp. 94–95, pp. 89–90).

In the revision, two pages dealing with Gollum's reactions as he passes Bilbo by, cursing and whispering about the Ring, are added. At the end, Bilbo realizes that the Ring is magical: "He had heard of such things, of course, in old old tales; but it was hard to believe that he really had found one, by accident." By the end of *The Lord of the Rings* we are aware that Bilbo's discovery is innocent though not accidental. After the addition, the narration picks up the original version again with a short transposition and then deals with the action when Gollum and Bilbo reach the end of the tunnel.

As they went along up the tunnel together, Gollum flip-flapping at his side . . .

He also learned that he ought to have turned down one of the side passages to the right before he came to the bottom . . .

On they went, Gollum flip-flapping ahead, hissing and cursing; Bilbo behind going as softly as a hobbit can. Soon they came to places where, as Bilbo had noticed on the way down, side-passages opened, this way and that.

Now on they went again, while Gollum counted the passages to left and right: "One left, one right, two right, three right, two left," and so on. He began to get very shaky and afraid as they left the water further and further behind;

but at last he stopped by a low opening on their left (going up)—"six right, four left."

"Here'ss the passage," he whispered. "It must squeeze in and sneak down. We dursn't go with it, my preciouss, no we dursn't, gollum!"

So Bilbo slipped under the arch, and said goodbye to the nasty miserable creature; and very glad he was. He did not feel comfortable until he felt quite sure it was gone, and he kept his head out in the main tunnel listening until the flip-flap of Gollum going back to his boat died away into the darkness. Then he went down the new passage (pp. 93–94).

Gollum began at once to count them.

"One left, yes. One right, yes. Two right, yes, yes. Two left, yes, yes." And so on and on.

As the count grew he slowed down, and he began to get shaky and weepy; for he was leaving the water further and further behind, and he was getting afraid. Goblins might be about, and he had lost his ring. At last he stopped by a low opening, on their left as they went up.

"Seven right, yes. Six left, yes!" he whispered. "This is it. This is the way to the back-door, yes. Here's the passage!"

He peered in, and shrank back. "But we dursn't go in, precious, no we dursn't. Goblinses down there. Lots of goblinses. We smells them. Ssss!"

"What shall we do? Curse them and crush them! We must wait here, precious, wait a bit and see."

So they came to a dead stop. Gollum had brought Bilbo to the way out after all, but Bilbo could not get in! There was Gollum sitting humped up right in the opening, and his eyes gleamed cold in his head, as he swayed it from side to side between his knees (p. 97, pp. 91–92).

The Leap in the Dark

In the original version Bilbo proceeds down the passage, but in the revision Tolkien introduces active evil in the form of the sentient Ring. This page and a half of new material increases the story's intensity because Bilbo must directly confront evil and its consequences. Bilbo is briefly transformed from the grumbling but good-hearted soul of *The Hobbit* into a heroic and compassionate individual. Evil has caused the downfall of Gollum, who is the subject of tragedy, of "endless unmarked days without light or hope" and Bilbo is the viewer of the drama, purged by pity and horror:

> Bilbo almost stopped breathing, and went stiff himself. He was desperate. He must get away, out of this horrible darkness, while he had any strength left. He must fight. He must stab the foul thing, put its eyes out, kill it. It meant to kill him. No, not a fair fight. He was invisible now. Gollum had no sword. Gollum had not actually threatened to kill him, or tried to yet. And he was miserable, alone, lost. A sudden understanding, a pity mixed with horror, welled up in Bilbo's heart: a glimpse of endless unmarked days without light or hope of betterment, hard stone, cold fish, sneaking and whispering. All these thoughts passed in a flash of a second. He trembled. And then quite suddenly in another flash, as if lifted by a new strength and resolve, he leaped. (p. 98, pp. 92–93)

The Aristotelian dimensions of Gollum's fate are so obvious that one is tempted to ignore them in a 'children's' story, yet they are unmistakable.

In the next paragraph of the revision, the terminology is so explicitly Christian and so commonplace in theological discussion that again one is tempted to assume that Tolkien has employed common expressions without thought. However, the serious meaning of the passage is inescapable. Having stayed his hand, Bilbo has refrained from evil. But he has still to save himself, to turn from the present evil and in the hope of salvation to leap into the dark:

> No great leap for a man, but a leap in the dark. Straight over Gollum's head he jumped, seven feet forward and three in the air; indeed, had he known it, he only just missed cracking his skull on the low arch of the passage. (p. 98, p. 93)

Faith: the leap in the dark that a man takes. Bilbo, a hobbit, takes it. The anticlimactic conclusion reinforces the Christian interpretation: man is a weak and insignificant creature who through faith and God's help overcomes insurmountable obstacles.

An additional half page follows, dealing with Bilbo's escape from Gollum, who chased him part of the way down the new passage, shrieking his despair and hatred. The passage is not necessary to *The Hobbit*, but it supplies the conflict in *The Lord of the Rings:* the everlasting enmity that exists between an evil creature with a maniacal desire for the Ring of Power and a compassionate protagonist who nonetheless comes by the Ring through theft.

After the heavy revision and expansion of the middle part of the chapter, Tolkien turns to a more subtle kind of revision for the remainder. It involves a slight degree of expansion—a sentence or two at a time, rather than paragraphs—and a few transpositions. It involves, too, the restatement of material that contradicts the meaning of the original.

In the earlier version of the following passage, Bilbo is reckless because he is still unaware of the goblins' physical superiority, but he still exercises "all care" because he perceives Gollum's nature. This shift in emphasis heightens the tension in their encounter. In revision of this passage Tolkien introduces the word *orcs*, which in the original edition occurred only in the name of the sword Orcrist. The sophisticated narrative techniques in subsequent sections of *The Lord of the Rings* are anticipated in this revision, first in his method of reintroducing the physical setting—the passage—after a lengthy digression and, second, by using discourse to carry meaning and emotional overtones, rather than depending entirely on exposition.

It was a low narrow one roughly made. It was all right for the hobbit, except when he stubbed his toes in the dark on nasty lags in the floor; but it must have been a bit low for goblins. Perhaps it was not knowing that goblins	The passage was low and roughly made. It was not too difficult for the hobbit, except when, in spite of all care, he stubbed his poor toes again, several times, on the floor. "A bit low for goblins, at least for the big ones," thought Bilbo,

| are used to this sort of thing, and go along quite fast stooping low with their hands almost on the floor, that made Bilbo forget the danger of meeting them and hurry forward recklessly (p. 94). | not knowing that even the big ones, the orcs of the mountains, go along at a great speed stooping low with their hands almost on the ground (p. 99, p. 93). |

A Last Trick of the Ring

The minor changes in the next section sharpen the visual quality to increase the tension of descriptive passages. The physical surroundings are given more texture in the revision: the passage has been sloping down before it begins to climb, and then climbs steeply; the passage turns a corner, then another corner, and then the last corner. The glimmer of light is intensified to a glimpse, connoting a brighter but briefer image and providing motivation for Bilbo's breaking into a run. Bilbo is no longer described in nursery-tale tones such as "scuttling along" on "little legs." The door, originally "left a little open," is now "left standing open."

| Soon the passage began to go up again, and after a while it climbed steeply. That slowed him down. But at last after some time the slope stopped, the passage turned a corner and dipped down again, and at the bottom of a short incline he saw filtering round another corner—a glimmer of light. Not red light as of fire or lantern, but pale ordinary out-of-doors sort of light. Then he began to run. Scuttling along as fast as his little legs would carry him he turned the corner and came suddenly right into an open place where the light, after all | Soon the passage that had been sloping down began to go up again, and after a while it climbed steeply. That slowed Bilbo down. But at last the slope stopped, the passage turned a corner, and dipped down again, and there, at the bottom of a short incline, he saw, filtering round another corner—a glimpse of light. Not red light, as of fire or lantern, but a pale out-of-doors sort of light. Then Bilbo began to run. Scuttling as fast as his legs would carry him he turned the last corner and came suddenly right into an open |

that time in the dark, seemed dazzlingly bright. Really it was only a leak of sunshine in through a doorway, where a great door, a stone door, was left a little open (p. 94).	space, where the light, after all that time in the dark, seemed dazzlingly bright. Really it was only a leak of sunshine in through a door-way, where a great door, a stone door, was left standing open (p. 99, pp. 93–94).

The open door, signifying escape, is an intentional and effective contrast to the elements next introduced in the revision: the "aroused, alert" goblins and the conscious, malignant Ring.

In the revision, the condition of the goblins emphasizes the active malevolence of the Ring. In the original version, Bilbo has given little thought to the ring; having been civilly directed to the exit by Gollum he walks through the passage, and when he encounters the goblin guards, he slips the ring on his finger—either by accident or presence of mind, but probably by the former, according to the narrator, who volunteers his opinion and the reason for it. In the revision, Bilbo, wearing the Ring, invisibly walks through the passage but, on encountering the guards, suddenly finds that he is visible and that the Ring is not on his finger. The narrator does not have a firm opinion: it may be accident or it may he a "last trick of the ring" before its acceptance of a new master. The narrator's uncertainty increases the importance of the Ring and stresses its evil nature, a characteristic not necessary or even appropriate to its original conception in *The Hobbit* but necessary to the theme developed in *The Lord of the Rings*.

Bilbo blinked, and then he suddenly saw the goblins: goblins in full armour with drawn swords sitting just inside the door, and watching it with wide eyes, and the passage that led to it!	Bilbo blinked, and then suddenly he saw the goblins: goblins in full armour with drawn swords sitting just inside the door, and watching the passage that led to it. They were aroused, alert, ready for anything.
They saw him sooner than he saw them, and with yells of	They saw him sooner than he saw them. Yes, they saw

delight they rushed upon him.

Whether it was accident or presence of mind, I don't know. Accident, I think, because the new treasure . . .

Anyway he slipped the ring on his left hand—and the goblins stopped short. They could not see a sign of him. Then they yelled twice as loud as before, but not so delightedly (pp. 94–95).

him. Whether it was an accident, or a last trick of the ring before it took a new master, it was not on his finger. With yells of delight the goblins rushed upon him.

A pang of fear and loss, like an echo of Gollum's misery, smote Bilbo, and forgetting even to draw his sword he stuck his hands into his pockets. And there was the ring still, in his left pocket, and it slipped on his finger. The goblins stopped short. They could not see a sign of him. He had vanished. They yelled twice as loud as before, but not so delightedly (pp. 99–100, p. 94).

The remaining page and a half of the chapter is the same in both texts: Bilbo manages to evade the guards and to squeeze through the slight opening left when the goblins push the door almost closed.

To summarize, then, Tolkien's chief alterations in 'Riddles in the Dark' change the stakes in the riddle-game, introduce the Ring as a ring of power—sentient, malevolent, addictive, and independent—define the opposing forces in the universe and convert Gollum from a simply lost creature to a totally depraved one. Any one of these changes could have been achieved in, at most, a few sentences, but the transformation of Gollum occupies most of the space devoted to revision.

Of the important transpositions, one concerns the properties of the Ring, one the distribution of side passages, and two concern Gollum: his search of the island and his flip-flapping along the tunnel.

The need for the first two kinds of revision are fairly obvious, but the changes in Gollum's character are as significant as they are interesting. The alterations clearly increase Gollum's role and remove the story from the realm of the nursery tale. The variety of techniques and the amount of space devoted to the transformation of character indicate that Tolkien attaches great importance to Gollum—more than is necessary or even suitable for his function in *The Hobbit.* But his prominence is appropriate to his expanded role in *The Lord of the Rings.*

NOTES TO CHAPTER 1

1. *The Hobbit: Or, There and Back Again* was well received by the reviewers when it was first published (London: Allen and Unwin, 1937; Boston: Houghton Mifflin, 1938) but ignored when the revised edition appeared (London, 1951; Boston, 1958). This revision was issued in paperback by Ballantine in 1966 to take advantage of the publicity attending the unauthorized Ace edition of *The Lord of the Rings*; the next year Ballantine issued a slightly revised edition which Tolkien was preparing for British publication (London: Longmans, Green, 1966).

2. First published 1954–56 (London and Boston), *The Lord of the Rings* consists of Part I *The Fellowship of the Ring,* Part II *The Two Towers,* and Part III *The Return of the King.* Ace Books brought out an unauthorized paperback edition in 1965 (Ace later reached an agreement with Tolkien to pay him royalties and not to reprint when current stocks were exhausted) and Ballantine Books countered in the same year with a paperback edition revised by Tolkien and containing an index and appendices. In 1967 the revised hardcover edition appeared (London and Boston) and was designated the second edition. In 1967 the British publishers came out with a one-volume paperback edition omitting the index and the appendices except for the Tale of Aragorn and Arwen.

3. '*Beowulf* and *The Hobbit:* Elegy into Fantasy in J.R.R. Tolkien's Creative Technique', unpublished doctoral dissertation (University of Southern California, 1969).

4. Philip Norman in 'The Prevalence of Hobbits', *New York Times Magazine* (Sunday, 15th January 1967) quotes Tolkien: "*The Hobbit* was written in what I should now regard as bad style, as if one were talking to children. There's nothing my children loathed more. They taught me a lesson. Anything that in any way was marked out in *The Hobbit* as for children, instead of just for people, they disliked—instinctively. I did too, now that I think about it" (p. 100).

5. Christopher Tolkien states in the introduction to *The Saga of King Heidrek the Wise* (London: Thomas Nelson, 1960) that "It has been pointed out that the contest in the saga shows affinity to a motif well known in fairy-tale literature, in which a prisoner gains his free-

dom by posing a problem which in its nature is insoluble," adding that "it is equally plain that it is inapposite as the last question of a riddle-match, since it is not a riddle" (p. xx). The motif is evident in 'Riddles in the Dark', as is the inappositeness of the procedure. Bilbo has qualms about deceiving Gollum but, of course, the good sense not to tell him the truth.

2

The Psychological Journey of Bilbo Baggins

DOROTHY MATTHEWS

Since its publication in 1938, J.R.R. Tolkien's *The Hobbit* has received very little serious attention other than as the precursor of *The Lord of the Rings*. It has usually been praised as a good introduction to the trilogy, and as a children's book, but anyone familiar with psychoanalysis cannot avoid being tantalized by recurrent themes and motifs in the three stories. Bilbo's story has surprising depths that can be plumbed by the reader who is receptive to psychoanalytic interpretations.

The central pattern of *The Hobbit* is, quite obviously, a quest. Like so many heroes before him, Bilbo sets out on a perilous journey, encounters and overcomes many obstacles (including a confrontation with a dragon) and returns victorious after he has restored a kingdom and righted ancient wrongs. However, this pattern is so commonplace in literature that it is not a very helpful signpost. But it may help in other ways.

Let us first look briefly at *The Hobbit* for its folk ingredients, that is, the common motifs or story elements which it shares with folk narratives. There are, of course, the creatures themselves: dwarves, elves, trolls, animal servants, helpful birds, and, the most frequently recurring of all folk adversaries, the treasure-guarding dragon. There are magic objects in abundance: a Ring of invisibility, secret entrances into the underworld, magic swords, and doors into mountains. Dreams foretell and taboos admonish, the violation of which could bring dire results.

There are tasks to be performed, riddles to solve, and foes to be outwitted or outfought. Folk motifs form the very warp and woof in the texture of this tale, which is not surprising since Tolkien, as a medievalist, is immersed in folk tradition, a tradition that gives substance not only to the best known epics but to most medieval narratives and to 'fairy tales'.

In fact, it is probably its resemblance to what today's readers see as the nursery tale that has resulted in *The Hobbit* being relegated to elementary school shelves. The fat, comfort-loving Bilbo can easily remind a reader of Winnie-the-Pooh, who had to have his "little something" at eleven o'clock or of another epicurean, Peter Rabbit, who risked all for a feast in Mr. MacGregor's garden. Bilbo's home-loving nature can also call to mind the domestic Water Rat and Mole of Kenneth Grahame's *Wind in the Willows*, for Bilbo found the sound of a kettle singing out to announce the hour for tea the most heartening in the world. And Bilbo's descent into the depths of the mountain where he loses track of time and finds himself confronted by menacing and riddling adversaries certainly bears a resemblance to *Alice's Adventures in Wonderland*. Bilbo can also be seen as similar to such diminutive heroes of international fairy tales as the master of 'Puss-in-Boots', 'Jack and the Beanstalk' and the endless stream of youngest of three sons who, through no outstanding qualities of their own, are propelled to riches and renown by the aid of magic objects or supernatural helpers.

But even if *The Hobbit* is only a children's story, it should be analyzed more closely for deeper levels of meaning, for it is the kind of story that has provided the most profound insights into the human psyche.

Initiation into Manhood

Both Freud's and Jung's studies of folk materials support the theory that the unconscious expresses itself through such channels as dreams and fantasy. The protagonist in so many of these tales encounters his greatest obstacles alone, as a dreamer. Even in large-scale epics the hero fights single-handedly although the stakes are much higher than in fairy tales. Beowulf confronts both Grendel and Grendel's mother alone, and Arthur and Mordred, as the only survivors on a corpse-strewn battlefield, decide the future of the kingdom through man-to-man struggle.

It is also suggestive that the descents in so many of these stories have a universal appeal. Trips into the underworld abound in Greek hero tales and myths as well as in Germanic lore. Just as Orpheus seeks Eurydice, just as Beowulf goes down into the sea to fight Grendel's mother in her lair, just as Alice falls into an underground realm, so Bilbo descends into the heart of the mountain to encounter Gollum and, later, Smaug. Freudian symbolism might also explain the prominence given in well-known tales to the nicknames of swords such as *The Hobbit*'s Orcrist (the Biter) and Glamdring the Foe-Hammer (the Beater), the acquisition of which is an important event in the life of the hero. Some of the most memorable episodes in the Arthurian tales are those describing Arthur's passing the test devised to identify the rightful king by miraculously freeing the sword from the stone, and his receiving the gem-encrusted Excalibur from the Lady of the Lake. If Freud's view of the sword as a phallic symbol is correct, then it does not seem far-fetched to view these scenes as vestiges of the coming-into-manhood ritual. Surely Freudian sex symbols are found with startling frequency in these stories. Recall, for instance, the prominence of keys, locks, caves, chalices, and cups in these works.

I can no more than touch upon this subject within the limitations of this chapter. Suffice it to say that the surprising and suggestive similarities in the narrative and image patterns of these tales, which have received the most universal human response, have been well documented by Jung and other psychologists. Jung's contention is that men respond to these stories because they are in effect one story, monomyth expressing in metaphor a psychic experience shared by all mankind. The perilous journey may indeed be seen as a poetic image for Everyman's passage through life. The obstacles met by the protagonist, though often in the form of confrontations with wondrous adversaries, may in fact represent mental rather than physical trials. In other words, such figures as dragons, monsters, spiders, and goblins may be externalizations of psychic phenomena which, contrary to general opinion, are far from unreal. Some of the most convincing evidence to support Jung's theory of archetypes has been the similarity between the creatures described in the world's literature and those depicted in the art of mentally deranged patients being treated by psychoanalysis.

The Individuation Process

In this light, the hero's quest may be viewed as a mirror of a quest for psychic wholeness as it is undertaken unconsciously by all human beings. Thus, recurring episodes in this frequently encountered narrative pattern may be interpreted as marking stages in what Jung calls the individuation process. Men may respond to these events because they are couched in the symbolic terms of the universal unconscious whereby they express the vital stages of maturation. Just as a hero is mysteriously summoned, often despite his initial reluctance, to undertake a journey beset by perils in order to find some treasure, so each individual must pass through crucial periods of trial at which times part of his former self must die so that a new and changed personality may emerge. A child must pass through puberty before reaching manhood. He must sever the ties with his past—specially with his mother—and he must die as a child in order to be reborn. The rite of becoming, still seen in primitive rituals by which a young boy is initiated into manhood through trials, symbolic deaths and rebirths, is also evident in these stories in the pattern of separation, initiation, and return. The fact that Tolkien subtitled *The Hobbit* as *There and Back Again* encourages this kind of reading. Let us then consider Bilbo Baggins's journey as a metaphor for the individuation process, his quest as a search for maturity and wholeness, and his adventures as symbolically detailed rites of maturation.

When we are first introduced to Bilbo, he is far from being a boy hobbit in terms of years, but his maturity is questionable. His primary concerns, like those of any child, are with physical comforts. Eating is probably his favorite activity. He seldom ventures from his hobbit hole, a dwelling interestingly womb-like in its isolation from the shocks of the world. Bilbo is noticeably annoyed when Gandalf arrives with the dwarf visitors since he would prefer to live what appears to be a somewhat withdrawn, self-centered life.

Early in the story it is clear, however, that Bilbo has much more in him than he is giving expression to. The potential for tension lies between the Baggins and the Took sides of his nature; through his mother, Belladonna Took, he is related to an adventurous family and has inherited aggressive tendencies. However, he has evidently repressed this more spirited side of his personality in favor of the Baggins impulses, which tend to be rather fuddy-duddy and more than a little feminine. Bilbo is much more interested, for instance, in keeping a tidy house, cooking a tempting meal, and keeping himself in pocket handkerchiefs than he is in venturing boldly into the world to find what life may have in store for him.

In other words, at the beginning of the tale, Bilbo's personality is out of balance and far from integrated. His masculinity, or one may say his Tookish aggressiveness, is being repressed so that he is clinging rather immaturely to a childish way of life. He has not even begun to realize his full potential. The womb-like peace and security of his home is disturbed with the arrival of Gandalf, who may be seen as a projection of the Jungian archetype of the Wise Old Man since he resembles the magic helper of countless stories: Merlin of the Arthurian cycle, Odin of Norse legend, or the helpful old person of the fairy tale, to name but a few. Like his prototypes, Gandalf sounds the call to adventure and motivates the reluctant hobbit to leave his home, helps him in the early stages of his venture into perilous realms, and then leaves him when he can stand alone.

Facing Danger Underground

At the outset of their adventure, Bilbo, like a typical young adolescent, is uncertain of his role, or 'persona', to use a Jungian term. The dwarves quickly reinforce his insecurity; Gandalf asked him to join the group to be a burglar, but the dwarves carp that he acts more like a grocer than a burglar.

He fears that he cannot live up to Gandalf's expectations, and during the early conflicts with the trolls and goblins, Bilbo is completely dependent upon the wizard for help. The most prominent force in these early events is luck, or chance. It is only through chance that the key to the trolls' cave is found, thus providing unearned access to the magic swords so necessary for later trials. If the sword is seen as a phallic symbol, its miraculous appearance at the beginning of the journey supports the ritualistic pattern of maturation in Bilbo's adventures.

One of the most crucial incidents of the story takes place when Bilbo finds himself unconscious and separated from the dwarves within the mountain domain of the goblins. In this underground scene he must face an important trial; he must make a decision whose outcome will be a measure of his maturity. After accidentally finding the Ring, Bilbo wonders whether or not he should summon up the courage to face whatever dangers await him. Unlike the unsure, regressive hobbit he was, Bilbo suddenly exclaims: "Go Back? No good at all! Go sideways? Impossible! Go Forward? Only thing to do!" For the first time Bilbo finds within himself a strength he didn't know he possessed. With unprecedented courage he decides to face life rather than to withdraw from it. This decision marks an important step in his psychological journey.

The danger he decides to face at this time, of course, is Gollum, the vaguely sensed but monstrous inhabitant of the underground lake. The association of this adversary with water and the attention given to his long grasping fingers and voracious appetite suggest a similarity to Jung's Devouring Mother archetype, that predatory monster which must be faced and slain by every individual in the depths of his unconscious if he is to develop as a self-reliant individual. The fact that the talisman is a Ring is even more suggestive of Jungian symbology since the circle is a Jungian archetype of the self—the indicator of possible psychic wholeness. The psychological importance of this confrontation is further supported by the imagery of the womb and of rebirth which marks the details of Bilbo's escape.

Wearing the Ring of invisibility, Bilbo finally makes his way to the exit from the subterranean realm of darkness only to find a menacing figure humped against the opening. The gleaming, cold green eyes tell him it is Gollum.

> Bilbo almost stopped breathing, and went stiff himself. He was desperate. He must get away, out of this horrible darkness, while he had any strength left. He must fight . . . And he was miserable, alone, lost . . . thoughts passed in a flash of a second. He trembled. And then quite suddenly in another flash, as if lifted by a new strength and resolve, he leaped . . . a leap in the dark . . . he only just missed cracking his skull on the low arch of the passage.

Narrowly missed by Gollum's desperate effort to grab him, Bilbo begins falling and lands in a new tunnel. The text continues:

> Soon the passage that had been sloping down began to go up again, and after a while it climbed steeply. That slowed Bilbo

down. But at last the slope stopped, the passage turned a corner and dipped down again, and there, at the bottom of a short incline, he saw, filtering round another corner—a glimpse of light. Not red light, as of fire or lantern, but a pale out-of-doors sort of light.

But Bilbo is no sooner out of the reach of Gollum when he is confronted by new dangers from the goblins. Here again the Ring helps him in his escape, which is described in terms highly suggestive of the traumatic natal experience:

> "I must get to the door, I must get to the door!" he kept saying to himself, but it was a long time before he ventured to try. Then it was like a horrible game of blindman's bluff. The place was full of goblins running about, and the poor little hobbit dodged this way and that, was knocked over by a goblin who could not make out what he had bumped into, scrambled away on all fours, slipped between the legs of the captain just in time, got up, and ran for the door.
>
> It was still ajar . . . Bilbo struggled but he could not move it. He tried to squeeze through the crack. He squeezed and squeezed, and he stuck! It was awful . . . He could see outside into the open air . . . but he could not get through. . . .
>
> Bilbo's heart jumped into his mouth. He gave a terrific squirm. Buttons burst off in all directions. He was through . . .

Bilbo Reborn

The suggestion of rebirth symbolically expressed in these passages is consistently carried out in the episodes that follow, and they clearly demonstrate that a metamorphosis has indeed taken place. When Bilbo rejoins his friends, he is unquestionably changed. The dwarves begin to notice a difference when, through the aid of his Ring, Bilbo is able to appear suddenly in their midst without detection, a feat much more befitting a burglar than a grocer. The delight and astonishment experienced by the dwarves is felt even more deeply by Gandalf, who is "probably more pleased than all the others."

> It is a fact that Bilbo's reputation went up a very great deal with the dwarves after this. If they had still doubted that he was really a first-class burglar, in spite of Gandalf's words, they doubted no longer.

The new respect which Bilbo has earned from his companions in turn leads to increased self-confidence; he is becoming a very different kind of hobbit. His decision to face danger has profoundly changed him.

The Tookish and Baggins sides of his personality have been brought into a new harmony. His Baggins impulses are beginning to be counter-balanced, thus bringing about a desirable psychic tension, which can result only when a balance of opposites exists. This is not the end of the journey, however, for the sudden change must be stabilized through reinforcing experiences. In fact, Gandalf remains with the party to see them through the adventure with the wargs and the goblins. It is during this episode that Gandalf summons help from the eagles, an act with possible symbolic significance since, according to Jung, the bird archetype is a powerful transforming agent. Similarly Beorn, with his interesting man-beast metamorphic possibilities, fits surprisingly well into Jung's conjectures regarding the archetypal figures of the unconscious.

The topography of the journey also has possible metaphoric significance. It is within a mountain reached through an underground descent that Bilbo finds the Ring and passes his first trial. It is now within a wood, Mirkwood, that Gandalf puts Bilbo in charge of the group. Woods have long been recognized as an archetype for danger, so Mirkwood is the appropriate setting for Bilbo to demonstrate his self-reliance. The wizard leaves his charge alone at the edge of the forest to face this next important test of manhood in the woods, and the spider finds Bilbo worthy of Gandalf's trust. He not only finds the courage to confront his adversary; he actually distinguishes himself by his valor. The monstrous enemy that threatens to hold and enmesh the hero in its web is a common metaphor for the paralysis of the victim, symbolically in a state of psychic fixation.

Escape from Paralysis

Whether the spider with whom Bilbo battles is interpreted as a Jungian shadow figure, embodying evil, or as the Devouring-Mother facet of the anima is immaterial. The symbolism is clear without specific terms: a lone protagonist must free himself from a menacing opponent that has the power to cripple him forever.

With the aid of a miraculously acquired sword and a magic talisman, he is able to face the danger and overcome it.

Let me present excerpts from Tolkien's description of this battle between Bilbo and the spider so that its details can become clear. Bilbo has found himself alone when the group's violation of the taboo forbidding their leaving the woodland path has resulted in their unexpected separation. The narrator tells us:

> That was one of his most miserable moments. But he soon made up his mind that it was no good trying to do anything till day came with some light, and quite useless to go blundering about tiring himself out with no hope of any breakfast to revive him. So he sat himself down with his back to a tree, and not for the last time fell to thinking of his far distant hobbit hole with its beautiful pantries.

So with this decision to regress into inactivity with "thoughts of bacon and eggs and toast and butter" to comfort him, Bilbo suddenly is alarmed by the touch of something up against him.

> Something like a strong sticky string was against his left hand, and when he tried to move he found that his legs were already wrapped in the same stuff, so that when he got up he fell over.
> Then the great spider, who had been busy tying him up while he dozed, came from behind him and came at him. He could only see the thing's eyes, but he could feel its hairy legs as it struggled to wind its abominable threads round and round him. It was lucky that he had come to his senses in time. Soon he would not have been able to move at all. As it was, he had a desperate fight before he got free. He beat the creature off with his hands—it was trying to poison him to keep him quiet, as small spiders do to flies—until he remembered his sword and drew it out. Then the spider jumped back, and he had time to cut his legs loose. After that it was his turn to attack . . .

Thus it is that Bilbo, during a temporary lapse into his old ways, is almost entrapped. However, decisive action, significantly taken by enlisting the aid of his sword, saves him, and he is able at last to kill the enemy with a clean stroke. The narrator's comments call attention to the change this encounter makes in Bilbo:

The spider lay dead beside him, and his sword-blade was stained black. Somehow the killing of the giant spider all alone by himself in the dark without the help of the wizard or the dwarves or of anyone else, made a great difference to Mr. Baggins. He felt a different person, and much fiercer and bolder in spite of an empty stomach, as he wiped his sword on the grass and put it back into its sheath.

And to commemorate the event, Bilbo declares: "I will give you a name, he said to it, his sword, "and I shall call you Sting." So with this name-bestowing ritual Bilbo himself underscores the symbolic import of the episode.

From this point on, Bilbo has the self-esteem needed to fulfill his responsibilities as a mature and trustworthy leader. It is through his ingenuity that they escape from the dungeon prisons in the subterranean halls of the wood-elves. This last episode also reveals telling symbolic details in that the imprisonment is underground and the escape through a narrow outlet into the water is yet another birth image.

Physical Courage: Slaying Smaug

The climactic adventures of Bilbo are of course the episodes with Smaug, who, like the traditional dragon of folklore, has laid waste the land and is guarding a treasure. If viewed in the light of Jungian symbology, the contested treasure can be seen as the archetype of the self, of psychic wholeness. Thus this last series of events marks the final stages of Bilbo's quest of maturation.

When the group arrives at the Lonely Mountain (another site aptly symbolic), it is noteworthy that it is Bilbo who prods the dwarves into beginning the dangerous search for the secret door. The helpful bird motif is again instrumental; this time, in accordance with the message read by Elrond from the moon letters on the map, the tapping of a thrush alerts Bilbo to look for the keyhole which is suddenly visible in the rays of the setting sun. The discovery of the door, swinging open with the turn of the key, presents the hobbit with his greatest challenge so far. Knowing that the dwarves expect him to be the one to explore the secret passage, Bilbo is ready with a response, even before he is asked:

. . . I have got you out of two messes already, which were hardly in the original bargain, so that I am, I think, already owed some reward. But third time pays for all as my father used to say, and somehow I don't think I shall refuse. Perhaps I have begun to trust my luck more than I used to in the old days.

Although his request for company on this dangerous mission is turned down, Bilbo nonetheless courageously enters through the enchanted door, steals into the mountain, puts on his Ring, and creeps noiselessly ". . . down, down, down into the dark. He was trembling with fear, but his little face was set and grim. Already he was a very different hobbit from the one that had run out without a pocket-handkerchief from Bag-End long ago. He had not had a pocket-handkerchief for ages. He loosened his dagger in its sheath, tightened his belt, and went on."

And so with this description, Tolkien makes it clear that Bilbo is facing his most demanding trial of physical courage by daring to descend alone into the dragon's lair. With every step, Bilbo feels internal conflict:

"Now you are in for it at last, Bilbo Baggins," he said to himself. "You went and put your foot right in it that night of the party, and now you have got to pull it out and pay for it! Dear me, what a fool I was and am!" said the least Tookish part of him. "I have absolutely no use for dragon-guarded treasures, and the whole lot could stay here forever, if only I would wake up and find this beastly tunnel was my own front-hall at home."

If he is ever to turn back, the time for it comes when his senses are assailed by the heat, the red light burning even brighter, and the terrifying sounds of bubbling and rumbling coming from the dragon hole. Tolkien describes this climactic moment:

It was at this point that Bilbo stopped. Going on from there was the bravest thing he ever did. The tremendous things that happened afterwards were as nothing compared to it. He fought the real battle in the tunnel alone, before he ever saw the vast danger that lay in wait.

From this point on, Bilbo's physical courage is unquestioned. It is true that his reputation flags a little when his first descent into the dragon's den touches off a devastating rampage, but he reasserts his leadership during the second descent by learning of the dragon's one vulnerable spot, the piece of information so vital in finally ridding the land of its menace. In the last descent Bilbo acquires the Arkenstone, the gem so important to both the elves and the dwarves. Again, it is significant to note that the incident incorporates Jungian symbols, for the problem presented by the Arkenstone results in a different kind of test for Bilbo. To solve it he needs moral rather than physical courage.

Only a Little Fellow After All

A truly critical question arises in considering this incident and the remainder of the story. I have taught this work many times and am constantly hearing complaints of dissatisfaction from students who feel that the last part of the book is both puzzling and anticlimactic. Many report that they felt a real loss of interest while reading the final chapters. Why does Bilbo keep the Arkenstone without telling the dwarves and then use it as a pawn in dealing with their enemies? Why, they ask, did Tolkien have a rather uninteresting character, rather than Bilbo, kill Smaug? Why is Bilbo, the previous center of interest, knocked unconscious so that he is useless during the last Battle of Five Armies? Isn't it a fault in artistic structure to allow the protagonist to fade from the picture during episodes when the normal expectation would be to have him demonstrate even more impressive heroism?

Answers to these questions are clear if the story is interpreted as the psychological journey of Bilbo Baggins. It stands to reason that Tolkien does not have Bilbo kill the dragon because that would be more the deed of a savior or culture hero, such as St. George, or the Red Cross Knight, or Beowulf. The significance of this tale lies in fact in the very obviously anti-heroic manner in which Tolkien chooses to bring Bilbo's adventures to a conclusion. As a result, Bilbo emerges as a symbol of a very average individual, not as a figure of epic proportion. Bilbo has not found eternal glory, but, rather, the self-knowledge that a willingness to meet challenge is not necessarily incompatible with a love of home. By giving expression to his Tookishness, he has found a new harmony and balance. And in realizing his full potential, Bilbo demonstrates that even his Baggins side provides him with values that are not without importance. Thorin recognizes this special worth in his final tribute to the hobbit:

> There is more in you of good than you know, child of the friendly west. Some courage and some wisdom, blended in measure. If more of us valued food and cheer and song above hoarded gold, it would be a merrier world.

Thus, at the conclusion of his adventures Bilbo finds the greatest prize of all: a knowledge of his own identity. In maturing psychologically, he has learned to think for himself and to have the courage to follow a course he knows to be right—in spite of possible repercussions. This maturity is demonstrated in the Arkenstone episode. His decision to use the gem as a means of negotiating with the opposition is made with the knowledge that it might mean the sacrifice of his friendship with Thorin and the dwarves. But Bilbo makes that choice. Like the hero in a medieval romance, he is confronted with a dilemma. Like Gawain, he has to face moral as well as physical trials. Bilbo makes the decision independently, trusting his own judgment and being willing to face censure and, if necessary, isolation. Bilbo's solution to this ethical problem satisfies Gandalf.

The initiate has survived all ordeals successfully. In achieving self-reliance and self-knowledge, he had indeed found the Jungian jewel hard to attain. And furthermore, Bilbo knows the role he was created to fill, for when Gandalf tells him: "You're a very fine person. . . . but you are only a little fellow in a wide world, after all," the hobbit answers simply, "Thank goodness."

3

The Fairy-tale Morality of *The Lord of the Rings*

WALTER SCHEPS

Considering the range and the emotional quality of critical reactions to *The Lord of the Rings*, a faint-hearted critic is tempted to seek refuge in arcana, such as tracking down the medieval counterparts to characters in the trilogy. For instance, Bombadil's wife, Goldberry, derives her name from the medieval romance *Havelock the Dane* and that fine young ent Quickbeam is merely a minor crux in an Old English glossary (the name Quickbeam means 'living tree' in Old English). Such investigations can be fascinating, especially to the trivia-lover in us, and the resulting book would certainly be a large one. Furthermore this approach is 'safe', which is no small consideration for a work which one critic has proclaimed comparable to *Moby-Dick*[1] and another has, with equal gusto, called "juvenile trash."[2] However, just what *The Lord of the Rings* is comparable to is, I believe, an important question, and it is one which I will attempt to answer in this chapter.

Perhaps the most salient characteristic of Tolkien's creation is that it is *his* creation: as Edmund Fuller says, "For this world he has created a self-contained geography, with maps, a mythology and balladry, a history in great depth and completeness of organization stretching back far behind the time-span of his story."[3] Fuller goes on to say that Tolkien has also created several languages. Actually Tolkien has created the illusion of having created several languages, a point I will take up shortly.

While Tolkien, like all authors, is accountable for his creation, his accountability, unlike that of most other authors, does not extend beyond that creation. We can expect Middle-earth to be internally consistent, but we cannot expect it to conform to important human values. Not only are the events and characters of the trilogy literally alien to us, but the means by which they are interpreted and the frames of reference into which they are placed are equally alien. Thus, when Tolkien tells us that hobbits "are (or were) . . . smaller than dwarves . . . but very much larger than lilliputians,"[4] we must understand that Tolkien is our exclusive source of information concerning these creatures; looking to our own experience for verification would be as perverse as it would be futile. Once we understand this distinction, we need no longer be bothered by the fact that Tolkien's evil creatures are black (orcs), speak ungrammatical, lower class English (trolls), come from the south and east (both orcs and trolls); and display an insatiable thirst for knowledge (Saruman and Sauron).

I do not mean to suggest that Tolkien's world is amoral (on the contrary, as Patricia Meyer Sparks has pointed out, "amorality is not really possible in Tolkien's scheme")[5] but rather that the morality which pervades the work, while not applicable only to itself, is nevertheless radically different from our own; and further, that any apparent similarity between the two moral systems is neither significant nor relevant to an understanding of *The Lord of the Rings*.

Places and Colors of Good and Evil

Middle-earth is morally charged; for instance, note Isabel C. MacCaffrey's term, "spatial cum moral dimensions,"[6] the physical with the moral dimensions, describing Tolkien's moral cartography in which North and West are generally associated with good, South and East with evil. In the northwestern part of Middle-earth, we have the Grey Havens from which the elves and Ring-bearers depart across the sea and, of course, the Shire. The northeast contains Mirkwood and what had been the Desolation of Smaug prior to the events described in *The Hobbit*, while Mordor, from which all evil in Middle-earth comes, is located in the southeast. The southwest quadrant is reserved for Gondor, whose placement suggests that realm's moral ambivalence, an ambivalence personified in the characters of Boromir and his father, Denethor. The Numenoreans, whose slow but inexorable decline has made possible the increasing power of Mordor, are from the Far West, Westernesse, or Numenor.

The focus of events in much of the trilogy is the Shire, and those events are most consistently described and interpreted by the Shire's residents, that is, from the hobbits' point of view. The Shire is divided into farthings or quadrants which are spatial and moral microcosms of Middle-earth at large. Thus, when Tolkien tells us that "away far east and south there were wars and growing fear" (I, p. 72)[7] and that "Fear seemed to stretch out a vast hand, like a dark cloud rising in the East. . . . (I, p. 81), we can expect that the Black Riders will appear first in the Eastfarthing (I, p. 112) and that Saruman's inroads into the Shire begin in the Southfarthing (II, p. 213). These moral dimensions hold, even in apparently incidental details. Bombadil advises the hobbits to pass the barrows on the west side only (I, p. 186), and when he continues to say that Bree's doors (I, p. 203) and windows (I, p. 206) look westward, we are psychologically prepared for the encounter with Strider, the representative of the True West.

A delicate but clearly defined balance is maintained between good and evil throughout the trilogy. Evil, for example, is consistently associated with blackness (Black Riders, I, p. 119; Black Breath, I, p. 231; Black Land, I, p. 322; Black Years, I, pp. 333–34; Black Shadow, I, p. 336); this association extends not only to descriptive detail (the orc chieftain in Moria is clad in black mail, I, p. 422, and the orcs employ black-feathered arrows, I, p. 500)[8] but also to the language which is used to describe evil. Thus, Treebeard calls Saruman "a black traitor" and says, somewhat redundantly, that if Saruman has succeeded in blending the races of orcs and men, that would indeed be "a black evil" (II, p. 96). And when Orthanc appears to Frodo like "a black spike" (I, p. 518), we know that Saruman is furthering the aims of Mordor even if he prefers to think of himself as being self-employed. If evil is associated with blackness, we would expect good to be described in terms of whiteness; and so it is. A symbolic indication of Saruman's treachery and hypocrisy is his abandonment of his white cloak in favor of an iridescent cloak of many colors (I, p. 339), and when Gandalf returns after his encounter with the Balrog, it is as Gandalf the White (II, p. 132).

Evil as Corruption

It is important to note that most of the distinctions between good and evil in *The Lord of the Rings* are generic distinctions, and the forces of evil are often immediately recognizable as such from their place of origin, their color, or their manner of speech. Tolkien's discussion of "The Black Speech" is significant in its implications concerning evil generally: "The Orcs were first bred by the Dark Power of the North in the Elder Days. It is said that they had no language of their own, but took what they could of other tongues and perverted it to their own liking; yet they made only brutal jargons, scarcely sufficient even for their own needs, unless it were for curses and abuse. And these creatures, being filled with malice, hating even their own kind, quickly developed as many barbarous dialects as there were groups or settlements of their race, so that their Orcish speech was of little use to them in intercourse between different tribes" (III, p. 511). The Orcish language, if such it can be called, then consists of words stolen from other languages and perverted for the orcs' own evil purposes. This linguistic phenomenon is very different from word borrowing. The orcs do not borrow words from other languages into their own; rather, they have no language except for what they are able to steal from others. And, of course, the distinction between theft and borrowing is basic to any moral system.

The perversion of language by orcs in the trilogy and by trolls in *The Hobbit* is the logical and inevitable consequence of the circumstances of their own creation, for as Treebeard tells Merry and Pippin ". . . Trolls are only counterfeits, made by the Enemy in the Great Darkness, in mockery of Ents, as Orcs were of Elves" (II, p. 113). In other words, the forces of evil are incapable of creating; they can only pervert and corrupt what is already there. This characteristic is often described in terms of the elemental conflict between nature and art. In the description of Isengard and the newly industrialized Shire, Tolkien emphasizes the foolish perversity and disastrous consequences of such attempts at improvement as the trolls' and orcs' creations. The Valley of Orthanc which "had once been green and fair . . . was now filled with pits and forges" (I, p. 341; cf. II, pp. 202–04) which are neither green nor fair, and Saruman, after he has left Isengard, is well on his way to turning the shire into a Mordorlike desert (III, p. 361).

Knowledge and Power Corrupt

For Nature to be corrupted in the manner described, her secrets must first be discovered. The pursuit of such knowledge is not only itself a manifestation of evil, but it provides the means by which evil enslaves others. Thus, we are told that Sauron ensnared the elven-smiths of Eregion through "their eagerness for knowledge" (I, p. 318), Saruman seeks to enlist Gandalf's services by promising him that they will gain "Knowledge, Rule, Order" (I, p. 340), and Elrond warns the members of the Council that "It is perilous to study too deeply the arts of the Enemy, for good or for ill" (I, p. 347). Perhaps the most definitive statement about the desire for knowledge, especially knowledge of Nature's secrets, is made by Gandalf to Frodo in their discussion of Gollum:

> All the 'great secrets' under the mountains had turned out to be just empty night: there was nothing more to find out, nothing worth doing, only nasty furtive eating and resentful remembering. (I, p. 87)

If knowledge of the kind represented by Sauron and Saruman is not to be trusted, what is to be trusted in *The Lord of the Rings* are precisely those sources of information which are not empirically verifiable and which have little applicability outside the confines of Middle-earth. First, old stories are to be trusted, as Sam says to Ted Sandyman (I, p. 73), Celeborn to Boromir (I, p. 484), Aragorn to one of the Riders of Rohan (II, p. 45), Gandalf to Theoden (II, p. 197), Sam to Frodo (II, pp. 407–411), and finally Tolkien to the reader (III, p. 518). Then, too, instinct and other vaguely defined forces are to be relied upon. Gandalf tells Frodo that he would have consulted Saruman but "something always held me back" (I, p. 78); he says that "Bilbo was meant to find the Ring, and *not* by its maker" (I, p. 88), and of Gollum says, "My heart tells me that he has some part to play yet, for good or ill, before the end . . ." (I, p. 93). Similarly, Frodo decides to leave the Shire on his and Bilbo's birthday because it "seemed somehow the proper day on which to set out . . ." (I, p. 99): needless to say, Frodo leaves just in time to escape the Black Riders. Bombadil's rescue of the hobbits in the Old Forest is no less fortuitous. "'Did I hear you calling? Nay, I did not hear: I was busy singing. Just chance brought me then, if chance you call it'" (I, p. 175). Tolkien's characters then are consistently being subjected to impulses of one kind or another, and for the most part these impulses, such as Sam's instinctive refusal to abandon Frodo in Cirith Ungol, are correct.

Instinctive reactions are crucially important in a world in which birds, plants, trees, and even the weather (as on Caradhras) may be part of the moral struggle between Good and Evil. Merry's comment on the Old Forest has universal applicability in Middle-earth: "Everything . . . is very much alive, more aware of what is going on . . . And the trees do not like strangers" (I, p. 156).

One of the ways in which Tolkien emphasizes the immediate moral immanence in *The Lord of the Rings* is the breaking down of the distinctions between words and the things they signify, especially his use of puns and verbal taboos. Some examples of puns are Goldberry's words to the hobbits in which she refers to "the ring in your voice" (I, p. 173); Strider's finding of "a beryl, an elf-stone" (I, p. 269) which, as we later learn, was left for Glorfindel; Elrond's speech to the council "What shall we do with the Ring, the least of rings that Sauron fancies? That is the doom that we must deem" (I, p. 318); and the description of the sound made by the orc drums in Moria as "Doom, doom" (I, p. 420). Verbal taboo operates exclusively on the forces of evil, and especially their names, the implication being that the names themselves are powerful sources of evil. Thus, Gandalf tells Pippin, "Evil things do not come into this valley, but all the same we should not name them" (I, p. 298) and warns Gimli not to name the Balrog (II, p. 133); Gollum refuses to name Cirith Ungol (II, p. 318); Anborn refers to "the shadow of the Unnamed" (II, p. 359; Pippin says that he will not speak of the Ringwraiths because they are near (III, p. 41); and the idea that proximity to evil makes it all the more necessary that it not be named is suggested too by Beregond, who says that the inhabitants of Gondor seldom refer to Mordor by name (III, p. 42). The power and danger in names is made clear by Gandalf who tells Frodo that Bilbo made the mistake of revealing his name to Gollum (I, p. 89) and that Frodo would do well therefore to conceal his own identity by travelling as "Mr. Underhill" (I, p. 97).

The refusal to name things is in effect a refusal to make use of knowledge and power and is not different in kind from

Gandalf's or Elrond's refusal to employ the Ring against Sauron. The uses of power in the trilogy, are, for the most part, strictly defined according to a rigid hierarchy and one of the most significant generic distinctions between good and evil is that the forces of Good abide by the limitations imposed upon them by the "natural" hierarchy while the representatives of Evil constantly seek to go beyond hierarchical restraints, and, by so doing, seriously disrupt the natural order.

The first disruption, as Tolkien tells us, occurred long before the events described in the trilogy. The "Ban of the Valar" had been laid upon the Numenoreans (III, p. 391), but as with Adam and Eve, "the more joyful was their life, the more they began to long for the immortality of the Eldar" (III, p. 391). Once the ban is broken, the Numenoreans begin to decline: "But in the wearing of the swift years of Middle-earth the line of Meneldil son of Anarion failed, and the Tree withered, and the blood of the Numenoreans became mingled with that of lesser men" (I, p. 321). There are indeed greater and lesser men in Middle-earth, masters and servants, kings and stewards; and their responsibilities and powers must be used according to the place of each in the natural hierarchy if that hierarchy, and indeed Middle-earth itself, are to survive. Nobility is inherited rather than acquired and is usually defined in terms of the office rather than the man who holds it. Thus, a steward of Gondor is a greater and more noble man than a king of Rohan, regardless of the identity of the particular individuals who occupy these positions. The reason, as Gandalf explains it to Pippin, is brutally simple: "Theoden is a kindly old man. Denethor is of another sort, proud and subtle, a man of far greater lineage and power, though he is not called a king" (III, p. 27). Like evil, innate nobility is easily and immediately recognizable. Thus Pippin senses that Faramir has "an air of high nobility such as Aragorn at times revealed, less high, perhaps, yet also less incalculable and remote: one of the Kings of Men born into a later time, but touched with the wisdom and sadness of the Elder Race" (III, p. 101): as Gandalf had said earlier, the "blood of Westernesse runs nearly true" in Faramir (III, p. 35). And Legolas bows before Aragorn because he instinctively recognizes "that here indeed was one who had elvenblood in his veins" (III, p. 181). The only egalitarian wind which blows through the sentient trees of Middle-earth comes from the East, and the egalitarianism of which it bears tidings is in foul slavery.

To be sure there are elemental forces at work in Middle-earth—forces like Bombadil and Shelob—which serve no master, but they too participate in the struggle between good and evil even if they seem to be indifferent to it. The characters who most nearly are morally ambivalent are Boromir and Gollum. The explanation of Boromir's behavior, his pride, vainglory, and selfishness, has already been alluded to: the blood of Westernesse does not run as truly in him as it does in his father and brother. And, since he dies well, the remaining eight walkers are inclined to make allowances for his earlier conduct, as I believe Tolkien wishes us to do.

Gollum, however, presents a more difficult problem. From the time he murders Déagol and steals the Ring, his entire existence revolves around his "precious" to the exclusion of all human, or hobbitlike, concerns. He is much more obsessed with the retention or the Ring than its use, and he is seduced primarily by its beauty rather than its power, the full extent of which he is never able to understand. However, flashes of Gollum's former self appear periodically, as in the riddle contest with Bilbo in *The Hobbit* and especially in the description of the perilous journey to Cirith Ungol. Gollum's two selves, which Sam calls Slinker and Stinker, counterpoint the struggle between good and evil, and the evil self wins out because of Sam's not entirely innocent intervention. Ironically, and significantly, Gollum's desire for the Ring leads to its destruction and his own and, of course, to the destruction of Mordor as well.

Evil Is Mightier than Good

That Mordor is literally destroyed from within is both aesthetically and morally appropriate. When Gandalf returns as the White Rider, he says, "I am Gandalf, Gandalf the White, but Black is mightier still" (II, p. 132). Evil is more powerful than good in Middle-earth for several reasons. First, evil seeks only to subvert and corrupt rather than create, a far more difficult task, and can make use of the hidden knowledge denied to the forces of good. And, too, evil has a tactical advantage because it has the initiative and can attack when and where it chooses.

Given these tremendous advantages, evil in *The Lord of the Rings* can be defeated, and then only temporarily, by turning its own devices against it. About Gollum, for example, Gandalf says to Pippin, "A traitor may betray himself and do good that he does not intend" (III, p. 108). Eomer says, "Our Enemy's devices oft serve us in his despite" (III, p. 133); and Aragorn says of Mordor, "With its own weapons was it worsted" (III, p. 186). Because evil is incapable of understanding good, it never occurs to Sauron that Gandalf will not use the Ring as he would if their situations were reversed. The Eye of Mordor turns inward, "trying to pierce the shadows that it had made for its own defense, but which now hindered it in its unquiet and doubt" (III, p. 213)—when it is too late.

At this point, it would perhaps be useful to summarize briefly the characteristics of good and evil as they are revealed in *The Lord of the Rings*. First, and most important, good and evil are almost always generically defined; we can often tell whether a character is one or the other if we know where he comes from, who his ancestors are, how he speaks, and which color, black or white, is associated with him. The evil characters pursue knowledge, especially technological knowledge, irrespective of the consequences of that pursuit, while the good characters trust both in their own goodness and in the innate perversity of evil as means to overcome it. If we attempt to transfer the moral values inherent in the trilogy to the 'real world', we find that they may be called paternalistic, reactionary, anti-intellectual, racist, fascistic and, perhaps worst of all in contemporary terms, irrelevant.

This does not mean that the moral values of *The Lord of the Rings* are unprecedented in literature. To cite some obvious parallels, we might note Hawthorne's distrust of unchecked scientific investigation, Spenser's use of the moral immanence of nature in *The Faerie Queene,* and Milton's employment of moral contraries, hierarchical moral structures, and the idea that evil invariably thwarts itself in *Paradise Lost*. We could, with Charles Moorman, cite the similarities in point of view between *The Lord of the Rings* and the Icelandic sagas[9] or concentrate on the striking resemblance between the ambivalent Christian morality of *Beowulf* and that found in Tolkien's work. But in each of these instances, we would, I believe, be mistaking the part for the whole. *The Lord of the Rings* as a whole is not really like any literary work, although it makes random use of various literary conventions and traditions.

The Hazardous Morality of Fairy Tales

The Lord of the Rings is similar to what we have become accustomed to calling 'fairy tales', although fairies rarely enter into them. Stories like 'Jack the Giant Killer (or 'Jack and the Beanstalk'), 'Hansel and Gretel', 'The Princess and the Pea', or even the naively vicious tale, 'The Jew Among Thorns', present exactly the same kinds of moral judgments which inhere in *The Lord of the Rings*. There are some difficulties in discussing these tales because each of them exists in a great many versions and no version is precisely like another. I shall concentrate, therefore, primarily on those narrative elements which are common to most versions.

Like Tolkien's trilogy, the fairy tale deals in moral absolutes, goodness in the fairy tale being associated with the young and the small, wickedness with the old and the big.[10] Most frequently, the characterization of good and evil in the fairy tale is a thinly veiled representation of the conflict involving children and parents; needless to say, in view of the fairy tale's popularity among them, the children invariably triumph. The tale of 'Jack the Giant Killer' is a perfect case in point. Virtually everything Jack does is, in terms of conventional morality, reprehensible. Jack initially disobeys his mother by squandering the money from the sale of the family's last salable item, a cow, on a packet of seeds which in some versions he purchases from a wizardlike figure. When the beanstalk miraculously appears the next morning, Jack decides to atone for his profligacy by climbing it into the realm of a wealthy giant. Of course, the giant has no name since he is defined generically; and, of course, the giant's wealth is ill-gotten, or so Jack has been told. Jack has been told too that the giant has severe cannibalistic tendencies; therefore, whatever methods Jack employs against him will be justifiable. To make a short story shorter, Jack secretes himself in the giant's castle, takes everything worth stealing while the giant is asleep, and when the giant attempts to reacquire his possessions, Jack murders him. For these barbarous and unnatural acts, Jack is acclaimed a hero. After all, it was only a giant.

'Hansel and Gretel' presents a somewhat similar situation. Lost in the woods and hungry, the two children come upon a gingerbread house which they proceed to ingest. The home-owner, a nameless witch, who is quite naturally disturbed by the children's actions, imprisons them and, admittedly, over-reacts by planning to put Hansel in the oven after she has sufficiently fattened him. Taking advantage of the old witch's failing eye-sight and her feebleness, Gretel, in a wonderfully insidious per-version of the Golden Rule, does unto the witch what the latter had planned to do unto Hansel. Thus, as in *The Lord of the Rings*, evil is overcome by its own devices, and the children rejoice; while the witch, who had earlier been undone, is now done in and, finally, overdone.

To say that the giant in the first tale and the witch in the sec-ond are stereotypes of evil is to miss the point, unless we are able to see the effect of such characterization. It would be fool-ish to become wildly indignant over Jack's treatment of the giant, but the witch in 'Hansel and Gretel' should at least make us uncomfortable; after all there were and are witches in the real world too, and the treatment which our ancestors accorded them was no different either in kind or degree from that employed by the children in the fairy tale. And if we substitute Jew or Black for Giant and Witch we can see that the major problem with fairy-tale morality is that we have not been con-tent to permit it to remain in the fairy tale. In the tale, 'The Jew Among Thorns' (a tale which appears in the Grimm collection of fairy tales but which is usually left out of American editions, for obvious reasons), the Jew is described in the same terms applied to giants and witches in the other stories. Like them, he is generically anonymous, and, like them too, he is generically evil. Can we accept what the fairy tale tells us about giants and witches and reject what it tells us about Jews? I think not, for when the events and characters of the fairy tale begin to appear in the real world, the fairy tale form itself ceases to exist: it comes to be construed either as prophecy or as propaganda.

A fairy tale like 'The Princess and the Pea' tells us that nobil-ity is literally skin deep and can be immediately perceived as such, while 'Rumpelstiltskin' says that it is permissible to break one's promise if the promise is made under duress to someone who is clearly alien and more than a bit peculiar. The reason that we are willing, even eager, to accept such simplistic and pernicious beliefs is precisely that they are simplistic and pernicious. As Aristotle said, man is a categorizing animal; and it is only natural that we should desire to make our categories as absolute as possible. Unfortunately, the complexity and diversity of the real world frustrate the categorizing impulse, and this frustration makes the morality of the fairy tale quite attractive. Giants, witches, and Jews, orcs, trolls, and goblins, all are generically evil. There are no exceptions, no individual instances to be pondered and weighed. Not only are all evil, all are immediately and physically recognizable as such. Within such a moral system there need never be any uncertainty about good and evil; as in 'The Jew Among Thorns', it is always as clear as the nose on one's face.

It is, I believe, indisputable that Tolkien is aware of all this in *The Lord of the Rings*. The very complexity and internal self-containment of Middle-earth make it virtually impossible to abstract any of it without seriously rupturing the whole, and the very alienness of the central characters—the hobbits—should indicate to us that the moral system which governs their world cannot, without serious consequences, be applied to our own. In many ways this system is identical to that of the fairy tale, but Tolkien has provided far more justification for it and has taken great pains to see to it that it remains sequestered in its own world. As Tolkien himself says in the foreword to *The Lord of the Rings*, ". . . I cordially dislike allegory in all its manifestations, and always have done so since I grew old and wary enough to detect its presence. I much prefer history, true or feigned, with its varied applicability to the thought and experience of readers. I think that many confuse 'applicability' with 'allegory'; but the one resides in the freedom of the reader, and the other in the purposed domination of the author" (I, p. xi). Or, in other words, 'Caveat lector'.

NOTES TO CHAPTER 3

1. W.H. Auden, 'The Quest Hero'. In Neil D. Isaacs and Rose Zimbardo, eds., *Tolkien and the Critics: Essays on J.R.R. Tolkien's The Lord of the Rings* (South Bend: University of Notre Dame Press, 1968, pp. 40–61), p.47. See also Charles Moorman, 'The Shire, Mordor, and Minas Tirith' (Isaacs and Zimbardo, pp. 201–117), p.201.

2. Edmund Wilson, 'Oo, Those Awful Orcs!', *The Nation*, 182 (14th April, 1956), pp. 312–14. Wilson's supposition that 'hobbit' is a blend of rabbit and Hobbs is perhaps overly ingenious. A blend of rabbit and hobby (as in hobbyhorse) seems to me far more likely.

3. 'The Lord of the Hobbits: Tolkien' (Isaacs and Zimbardo, pp. 17–39), p. 17.

4. *The Hobbit: Or, There and Back Again* (New York: Ballantine Books, 1965), p. 16. All references are to this edition. The lower case 'l' of "lilliputians" is significant; Tolkien here is not making a literary allusion.

5. 'Power and Meaning in *The Lord of the Rings*' (Isaacs and Zimbardo, pp. 81–99), p. 93.

6. *Paradise Lost as Myth* (Cambridge, Mass.: Harvard, 1959), p. 55.

7. I, II, and III refer to the three volumes of *The Lord of the Rings* in the Ballantine edition (New York, 1968).

8. We also have references to "black men" (for example I, p. 228), "the Morannon" or "Black Gate" (II, p. 309; III, p. 200), "the Black Hand" (II, p. 311), "the Black One" (II, p. 318), and "Black Numenoreans" (for instance III, p. 202). Needless to say one of Pippin's Orcish guards carries a "black knife" (II, p. 59).

9. 'The Shire, Mordor, and Minas Tirith' (Isaacs and Zimbardo, pp. 201–217. See also, Moorman's '"Now Entertain Conjecture of a Time": The Fictive Worlds of C.S. Lewis and J.R.R. Tolkien', in Mark R. Hillegas, ed., *Shadows of Imagination: The Fantasies of C.S. Lewis, J.R.R. Tolkien, and Charles Williams* (Carbondale: Southern Illinois University Press, 1969), pp. 59–69.

10. Cf. Frodo's statement that before he met Strider he thought that all "Big People" were "just big, and rather stupid" (I, p. 291).

4

The Corruption of Power

AGNES PERKINS and HELEN HILL

The Lord of the Rings has been interpreted by critics as a modern epic, as 'merely' an adventure story, as allegory (both Christian and contemporary), and even as a didactic fable of good and evil. Tolkien has stated explicity that it is not an allegory, and that he in fact dislikes allegory; on the other hand it certainly is an adventure story, it does have some epic qualities and it is concerned with the conflict between good and evil. But if one takes its thematic qualities seriously, it specifically seems to be a study in power, especially in the evil that accompanies the desire for power. The central question posed in the book is a moral one: What does the possibility of unlimited power do to the one who desires it, even to the one who desires it for good ends? And the answer is unequivocal: The desire for power corrupts.

Tolkien does not simply tell us this once; a series of characters and incidents throughout the book explores the effects of power on characters strong and weak, good and evil, great and humble. He also shows us those to whom the possibility for power means nothing because they have removed themselves from the conflicts of the world. And finally, with the return of the true king, he shows us how power may come to one who has the inherited right but achieves it only after he has resisted the desire for unearned power. It is as though seeing the same gem from each of its many facets, we perceive the same truth.

The Ring itself is the epitome of power, the One Ring, forged by Sauron to control the other rings held by elves, men, and dwarves and lost by Sauron after his defeat in battle centuries before:

> Three Rings for the Elven-kings under the sky,
>> Seven for the Dwarf-lords in their halls of stone,
> Nine for Mortal Men doomed to die
>> One for the Dark Lord on his dark throne
> In the Land of Mordor where the Shadows lie.
>> One Ring to rule them all, One Ring to find them,
>> One Ring to bring them all and in the darkness bind them
> In the Land of Mordor where the Shadows lie. (I, pp. 59–60)

The Ring can make its wearer invisible, as Bilbo discovered in *The Hobbit*. But more important, it can keep its wearer ageless and unchanged, it can control the power of the other rings and to some degree its own destiny, and most dangerous of all, it will corrupt its user. This quality, of course, determines the central plot, since the Ring cannot be used for good and can be destroyed only by returning it to the place of its forging, the fires of Mount Doom in Mordor, the realm of the Dark Lord, Sauron himself. This is the almost hopeless mission of the party of nine which sets out from Rivendell. Of these nine, four are never really concerned with the central question of the power of the Ring: Legolas the elf, Gimli the dwarf, Merry and Pippin, young hobbits related to Frodo, all are involved in important action in the story; but they are essentially follow-ers, neither desiring to rule or lead, nor forced into a position where they must take charge. They do not, therefore, desire the Ring and are not subject to its corruption, but each of the other major characters is revealed in relation to the temptation of the Ring.

These major characters seem to fall into groups of three. First, there are the three already wholly corrupted by the desire for power—Sauron, the Ringwraiths, and Gollum. Second, there are the three who belong to an earlier time and have removed themselves from the world to such a degree that the power of the Ring means nothing to them—Shelob, Fangorn, and Tom Bombadil. Third, there are the three, The Great, who would have the strength to wield the power of the Ring if they did obtain it—Saruman, Gandalf, and Galadriel. Fourth, there are the three men of Gondor to whom the Ring offers special temptation in their threatened land—Boromir, Denethor, and Faramir. And fifth, there are the three who for differing reasons obtain heroic stature in the story—Frodo, Sam, and Aragorn.

Of the three already corrupted by the desire for power, the strongest, the most evil, is Sauron the Dark Lord, who never appears in the book except in the minds and conversation of others. Sauron is unrelieved evil; however, even Sauron was not always evil, Elrond points out. "For nothing is evil in the beginning." For ages past, however, Sauron has desired to control the world for evil and at great cost has been defeated but never destroyed. His fair bodily form was destroyed during the wreck of Numenor in the second age, but he returned as "a spirit of hatred borne upon a dark wind" and afterwards became black and hideous and ruled through terror.

"Always after a defeat and a respite," Gandalf tells Frodo, "The Shadow takes another shape and grows again" (I, p. 60). Sauron's power depends on his control of the Ring because he forged it to control the other sources of power, and he poured much of his original strength into it. With it he will gain control of the world, but if the Ring is destroyed he may be crippled forever.

Sauron's chief servants have also been corrupted by the lust for power. These are the nine Black Riders, the Ringwraiths or Nazgûl, who were Numenorians but, in their desire for power, long ago became Sauron's vassals in exchange for the nine rings that were forged for mortal men. In his service they have become utterly subject to his will and reduced to terrible inhuman spirits of malice, whose very shadows strike despair into men's hearts. On the battlefield outside Gondor, Merry sees one of the winged creatures, bearing a Ringwraith, as it approaches to attack Theoden, king of the Mark:

> Down, down it came, and then, folding its fingered webs, it gave a croaking cry, and settled upon the body of Snowmane, digging in its claws, stooping its long naked neck.
> Upon it sat a shape, black-mantled, huge and threatening. A crown of steel he bore, but between rim and robe naught was there to see, save only a deadly gleam of eyes: the Lord of the Nazgûl. (III, p. 115)

The most complex character to succumb completely to the desire for power is the loathsome creature from *The Hobbit*, Gollum, from whom Bilbo contrived to take the Ring in the tunnels of the orc mountain. How Gollum first came to have the Ring is a long story. We do know that he had murdered to get it, and that through it he had lost his former name, Sméagol, and most of his identity and for many years had been hiding in the deepest caverns of the mountain trying to protect his "precious." Gollum was the Ring's slave when he lost it to Bilbo and his craving for it has driven him to trail it for many years, trying in vain to regain it. Although he has been too weak to use the Ring for his own ends, except for catching goblins, his tenacity (perhaps a remnant of his ancestry—he is related to an early branch of the hobbits) has kept him from being utterly destroyed. When he finally catches up to Frodo and Sam and is overcome while attempting to kill them and take the Ring, Frodo pities him and allows him to stay with them. Frodo also makes him swear on the Ring not to harm them, the oath being by the one thing Frodo knows will bind Gollum. Thereafter Gollum is torn between his desire for the Ring and its power over him, until he becomes a split character—Gollum, who would strangle Frodo to get the Ring, and Sméagol, who is bound by the power of the Ring not to harm the hobbits. He even holds debates with himself, speaking in the third person and referring to Sauron as "He":

> "But the precious holds the promise," the voice of Sméagol objected.
> Then take it," said the other, "and let's hold it ourselfs! Then we shall be master, *gollum*! Make the other hobbit, the nasty suspicious hobbit, make him crawl, yes, *gollum*!"
> "But He'll see, He'll know, He'll take it from us!"
> "No, sweet one. See, my precious: if we has it, then we can escape, even from Him, eh? Perhaps we grows very strong, stronger than Wraiths. Lord Sméagol? Gollum the Great? *The* Gollum! Eat fish every day, three times a day, fresh from the Sea. Most Precious Gollum! Must have it. We wants it, we wants it, we wants it!" (II, pp. 240–41)

An interesting contrast is provided in the next three characters, all of whom have withdrawn from the world and are untouched by the desire for power: Tom Bombadil, the master of the Old Forest; Treebeard (or Fangorn) of the ents; and Shelob, the monstrous, ancient spider who dwells in the tunnel at Cirith Ungol. Of these, Shelob is unquestionably evil, in her own way as wicked as any of the first three groups, but her only interest is in food for herself. Gollum is confident that she will cast away the Ring with Frodo's clothes when she eats him because her sting gives her enough power to satisfy her only desire.

Treebeard, or Fangorn, oldest of the ents, belongs to a slowly dying race of tree-herds, slowly dying because they have lost their wives and so have no young, no entings, and also because they are themselves becoming more 'treelike'. They help destroy Saruman because their wrath has been aroused by the hewing and chopping of the orcs. But they are much too old to have any real interest in the affairs of the rest of the world or to desire power for themselves.

Tom Bombadil, too, is old—"eldest," he calls himself; yet he is forever young, a merry, singing, forgetful fellow, in complete control within his own territory, but no longer willing to step outside his self-imposed boundaries. When the four hobbits are in his house in the Old Forest, he suddenly says, "Show me the precious Ring," and Frodo hands it over to him without question. There are only three other times that a character parts with the Ring of his own accord: when Bilbo leaves the Ring to Frodo, when Frodo hands it to Galdalf at Bag End, and when Sam gives it back to Frodo in the orc tower at the edge of Mordor. Tom plays with it a minute, then slips it on and does not disappear. Moreover, when, after he has given it back, Frodo tries it on to test it, the other hobbits find him invisible hut Tom still sees him clearly. Frodo can freely give the Ring to Tom because it does not have any power over him, or for him. For Tom is "Master of wood, water, and hill," but he is not burdened owning it; he has no fear, but he also has no sense of responsibility. At the council in Rivendell the hobbits discuss taking the Ring to Tom Bombadil for safekeeping, but they decide against it. "He would not understand the need," Gandalf says,

> And if he were given the Ring, he would soon forget it, or most likely throw it away. Such things have no hold on his mind. He would be a most unsafe guardian. (I, p. 279)

Although the three Great Ones, Gandalf, Galadriel, and Saruman, are not so old as Bombadil, Shelob, and Treebeard, they have spanned the ages. Saruman is the only one who succumbs to the desire for power. He is misled into thinking that he can avoid being corrupted if he joins the Enemy for his own good ends. Because he has the wisdom and strength which might have saved him, his failure to resist the temptation is most deplorable. At just what point temptation has taken possession of him is not clear, for he has been very great among the Wise and is extremely clever at concealing and persuading. He has established his kingdom at Isengard and treacherously made an alliance with Sauron, yet at the same time has plotted and schemed to obtain the Ring and become greater than even Sauron. His mistake lies in trying to subvert Gandalf to get the Ring. "A new power is rising," he tells Gandalf.

> As the power grows, its proved friends will also grow; and the Wise, such as you and I, may with patience come at last to direct its courses, to control it. We can bide our time, we can keep our thoughts in our hearts, high and ultimate purpose: Knowledge, Rule, Order; all the things that we have so far striven in vain to accomplish, hindered rather than helped by our weak or idle friends. (I, p. 272)

When Gandalf protests that this is madness, Saruman cannot conceal a lust which shines suddenly in his eyes. "Why not, Gandalf? . . . Why not? The Ruling Ring? If we could command that, than the Power would pass to us" (I, p. 273).

Gandalf absolutely rejects such a proposal from Saruman, for he sees through the pretense to Saruman's real ambitions; but, more important Gandalf rejects the Ring when Frodo, first learning of its power and protesting that he has too little will and wit for such a care, suggests in his innocence that Gandalf take it. The passionate strength of Gandalf's refusal suggests the strength of the temptation.

> "No," cried Gandalf, springing to his feet. "With That power I should have power too great and terrible. And over me the Ring would gain a power still greater and more deadly." His eyes flashed and his face was lit as by a fire within. "Do not tempt me! For I do not wish to become like the Dark Lord himself. Yet the way of the Ring to my heart is by pity, pity for weakness and the desire of

strength to do good. Do not tempt me! I dare not take it, not even to keep it safe, unused. The wish to wield it would be too great for my strength. I shall have such need of it. Great perils lie before me." (I, pp. 70–71)

Just as clearly Galadriel, lady of the elves of the Golden Wood, sees what would happen if the Ring came into her hands. Her temptation lies not so much in her concern for the people of Middle-earth as in her own position as an elven queen, because if the Ruling Ring is destroyed, the three rings held by the elves, one of which she wears, will lose their power and the time of the elves will grow short. They will have to leave Middle-earth for the realm of the West, over the sea. Finding her wise, beautiful, and fearless, and feeling unequal to the task he has attempted, Frodo offers the Ring to her. She has often wondered what she would do if the Ring should come within her grasp. For a moment even this idealized lady of the high elves is tempted. "In place of the Dark Lord you will set up a Queen. And I shall not be dark, but beautiful and terrible as the Morning and the Night . . . All shall love me and despair!" Then she laughs and says in a soft, sad voice, "I pass the test. I will diminish, and go into the West, and remain Galadriel" (I, p. 381).

To the men of Gondor the Ring offers a special temptation. Their country is directly west of Mordor and has been its chief enemy for many years. As the power of Mordor has grown, so the need for some great strength in Gondor has become more desperate. Boromir, the elder son of Denethor, lord and steward of the city of Gondor, is the first to be tempted. He is as strong and valiant as his brother Faramir but, like his father, proud and rash. When he first hears of the Ring at the council at Rivendell, he urges using it as a weapon against Sauron, but he is silenced by Elrond. During the early part of the journey of the Fellowship, his stamina and bravery are beyond question, yet as they approach Gondor the idea of gaining possession of the Ring begins to gnaw on him. Sam notices how his eyes pursue Frodo intently. When Frodo is alone trying to work up his courage to go off toward Mordor, Boromir follows him and tries to persuade him that the Ring has been sent for the defense of Gondor. "It is mad not to use it," he says, "to use the power of the Enemy against him. The fearless, the ruthless, these alone will achieve victory . . . The Ring would give me power of

Command. How I would drive the hosts of Mordor, and all men would flock to my banner." When persuasion fails, Boromir furiously tries to take the Ring from Frodo by force. Frodo escapes by putting the Ring on, thereby becoming invisible, and almost immediately Boromir is aware of the immensity of the wrong he has done. His character is at least partially redeemed when he dies defending Pippin and Merry from attacking orcs.

Boromir's death is a terrible blow to proud old Denethor, but the realization that his other son, Faramir, has actually had the Ring within his grasp yet has refused to seize it is almost more than he can bear. He berates Faramir as an unworthy soldier, a wizard's pupil, and he bemoans the fact that it is Faramir who lives when Boromir was the truer son. Denethor's pride brings about his own destruction. The Ring fortunately does not come within his grasp, but he challenges Sauron by gazing into the *palantír* of Minas Tirith, is driven mad by the evil force of Mordor, and dies in the flames of a funeral pyre of his own making.

Of the men of Gondor, only Faramir, who has studied with Gandalf, understands the danger of the Ring. When he meets Frodo and Sam in the forests of Ithilien, he guesses, even before Sam unwittingly blurts the secret, that they are bearing the Ring to its destruction. He tells them he knows the power of the heirloom they bear, but that even if he found it he would not dare to try to use it for the defense of Gondor. When he learns their full story, he repeats, "Not if I found it on the highway would I take it . . . I am wise enough to know there are some perils from which a man must flee."

Aragorn, Sam, and Frodo can each be seen as the hero of the hook. Each of them is given a particularly persuasive reason for using the Ring. Frodo, of course, is the main Ring-bearer, the chief protagonist of the book, and most obviously heroic, but he is the unlikely hero who does not seek to do great deeds and has no idea that he will have the strength to perform the task which circumstances force upon him. At the council at Rivendell, after all the possibilities of action have been discussed, no one volunteers to carry the Ring into the land of Mordor except old Bilbo, whose offer is respectfully but fondly rejected because of his age. There is a long silence.

> Frodo glanced at all the faces, but they were not turned to him. All the Council sat with downcast eyes, as if in deep thought. A

great dread fell on him, as if he was awaiting the pronouncement of some doom that he had long foreseen and vainly hoped might after all never he spoken. An overwhelming longing to rest and remain at peace by Bilbo's side in Rivendell filled all his heart. At last with an effort he spoke, and wondered to hear his own words, as if some other will was using his small voice.

"I will take the Ring," he said, "though I do not know the way." (I, p. 284)

It is important that the burden is not forced upon him. He accepts it freely though not eagerly, but he is never confident that he will accomplish his mission. As they get nearer to Mount Doom, the Ring becomes a dragging weight which makes him stagger, and it gains an increasingly strong hold on his mind. "I see it in my mind all the time," he tells Sam, "like a great wheel of fire." It also begins to dominate his will. After Sam has just trailed him to the tower of the orcs and planned his escape, he tells Frodo that earlier he took the Ring. Frodo wildly demands it back and calls him a thief. Although he is immediately sorry, it is apparent that the Ring is gradually gaining possession of him. When, after overcoming almost impossible obstacles, they finally reach their destination, the reader is shocked but hardly surprised that the temptation has been too much for Frodo and that he cannot, or will not, give up the Ring. "I have come," he says, "but I do not choose now to do what I came to do. I will not do this deed. The Ring is mine!" It is only by the strange, unlooked-for but completely appropriate intervention of Gollum that the mission can finally be accomplished (III, p. 223).

Sam Gamgee is without question one of the most lovable characters in Tolkien's works. He serves as the practical, clear-eyed realist who repeatedly brings any high-flown or overtense situation back firmly to earth. At the edge of Mordor he finds himself in a predicament he did not foresee, with Frodo apparently dead and the Ring still a very dangerous distance from the cracks of Mount Doom. So Sam becomes the Ringbearer, determined for better or worse to try to take it to its destruction. Sam's temptation by the Ring is strong, for he actually has it in his possessions, but it is short-lived. When he first comes out east of the mountains and looks on the terrible waste and desolation of Mordor, his heart returns to his profession, gardening, and he desires the power of the Ring to make all this foul land into a garden:

Wild fantasies arose in his mind; and he saw Samwise the Strong, Hero of the Age, striding with a flaming sword across the darkened land, and . . . at his command the vale of Gorgoroth became a garden of flowers and trees and brought forth fruit. He had only to put on the Ring and claim it for his own, and all this could be.

In that hour of trial it was the love of his master that helped most to hold him firm; but also deep down in him lived still unconquered his plain hobbit-sense . . . The one small garden of the free gardener was all his need and due, not a garden swollen to a realm. (III, p. 177)

The climax of the story, in fact most of the Sixth Book, is seen through Sam's eyes. Sam has been described as the only true hero of the book, because he alone gives up the Ring willingly, but even he feels some reluctance at the end.

When Aragorn joins the hobbits in Bree, he is introduced as Strider, the grim ranger who travels in the wilderness and patrols the far borders of the distant lands. We learn only gradually that he is Aragorn, Isildur's heir, the true king of Gondor; and only gradually too do we learn how great and noble he is. Aragorn, more than anyone else in the book, fits the mold of the epic hero; yet for all his dignity, there is a warmly human side to his personality. He banters with Merry in the House of Healing, he is grieved that he cannot return Éowyn's love, and he is deeply troubled when he fears he has failed Gandalf at Parth Galen. He inherits the job of leading the fellowship after Gandalf becomes lost in the Mines of Moria, of leading the host of the dead to the battle of Pelargir and finally leading the forces of Gondor to challenge the might of Mordor. The possibility of taking and using the Ring is continually before him, but his understanding is so deep and his nobility so great that he is never really tempted.

And in the long run Aragorn is the only one who achieves any real power. The hobbits do have a certain power of personality which permits them to lead in making short work of the ruffians, but it is no more than the product of their experiences. Aragorn, becoming the High King, has extensive power, but it is important that this comes to him through hereditary right as well as long years of patient effort and great valor. How much of this right to rule is a reflection of Tolkien's royalist sympathies is debatable. His attitude may be royalist, but it is also realistic. Although he distrusts power, he does not advocate weakness, or any compromise with evil, or pacifism in the face of an aggressive enemy. Aragorn uses the forces that he can legitimately command from Gondor and Rohan, from the Dúnedain, and even from the Dead—all of whom owe him their allegiance because of who he is, but also because of what he has done. He has earned the moral right which, of course, carries with it the responsibility to use his position justly and humanely. He is great because he has steadfastly fought against evil, not because he has set out to seek power.

Since the early thirties, when Tolkien began writing, we have witnessed the rise to power of great and terrible forces. Today we are hearing demands for power from every side, ever more shrill and imperative, with scarcely a voice raised to question the value of power, to point out its dangers to the power-wielder himself, to warn of its temptations. Yet what Tolkien is saying about power is not just advice for our times. It draws on a familiarity with the wisdom of centuries of literature and history and is relevant to any age, and (as he shows us through a great variety of characters) to any sort of man. And he says it clearly and without compromise: beware of power. The desire for power corrupts.

5

Everyclod and Everyhero: The Image of Man in Tolkien

DEBORAH C. ROGERS

I am always grateful when people giving papers say at the beginning what their point is, so I shall do so. I intend to show that there is another aspect of Man-as-presented-by-Tolkien in addition to the aspect we are all conscious of. What we all know is that hobbits are Tolkien's 'normal people' *par excellence*: the race and kind of character from whose point of view we see the doings in which we become involved. What I should like to add is a suggestion that Aragorn is also the representative of Man in Tolkien's stories, though we can see at a glance that he is in a different class of being from the hobbits.

Let us begin by considering hobbits because they are central to Tolkien's picture of humanity, a fact which has been recognized by others.[1] But first, I will discuss briefly the races in *The Lord of the Rings*. Tolkien's hobbits certainly are not human beings. He presents us in fact with seven 'speaking peoples': hobbits, elves, dwarves, ents, orcs, trolls, and men, each a separate race.

However, at least some of these races can intermarry. Tolkien tells us there have been three elf-human marriages (III, p. 338).[2] At the Battle of the Hornburg, some of Saruman's forces seem to be orc-human halfbreeds (II, p. 180). There is also the rumor in *The Hobbit* that once a Took had "married into a fairy family (the less friendly said a goblin family)" (p. 16).[3] 'Goblin' means orc, and it is still occasionally so used in *The Lord of the Rings*.

On the other hand, 'fairy' is a word Tolkien uses so little in his tales of Middle-earth that one surmises he is consciously avoiding it because of the connotations of triviality the word has picked up. But the wonder and greatness of 'faery' are present in *The Hobbit* and *The Lord of the Rings* and are carried by the elves.

Therefore I conclude as follows: that 'fairy' in the language of Middle-earth was a word used for elves—by hobbits who didn't believe in elves. These would be the provincial-minded hobbits of the period Tolkien is writing about (SR 1340ff.). The reader will perceive it as in the highest degree unlikely that any hobbit ever married an orc or an elf, but it seems to be not totally inconceivable genetically, whatever it may be in terms of character.

But what is the nature of character in Tolkien's trilogy? We have seen that Middle-earth has seven intelligent races, besides other odd beings, different and distinct though not all genetically incompatible. But Tolkien is one of us: a member of the race of men, in the twentieth century after Christ. And we only know one intelligent race: our own. The three divisions of human beings which we call 'races' are merely subdivisions of one basic kind of being.

Since we only know one kind of intelligent being, our imagination is limited. We have only one kind of experience to draw on in trying to portray persons of other races. What we do, therefore—what any author trying to show other beings does—is to use aspects of the one rational race we do know. And of course our one race does have as many different aspects as one could wish. Partly, then, Tolkien's seven different races are aspects of man. (I will be coming back to what C.S. Lewis said about that.)

And, to return to what I was saying, the hobbits are the race *par excellence* in *The Hobbit* and *The Lord of the Rings*. One can tell this in part because Tolkien uses their point of view, but even more because he obviously likes them very much indeed, and without evading their shortcomings in his portrayal. *I* can also tell from a letter which Tolkien sent me in 1958, in which he said, "I am in fact a hobbit."

So what are hobbits like, these original and most important creatures of Tolkien's? Their main qualities are apparent: they are small, provincial, and comfort-loving.

Some people add to these essential qualities that hobbits are utterly English. I raise the point only to refute it. Of course Tolkien is English; his experience, sentiments, and his literary heritage are English, so his expression is in the English idiom. However, to regard hobbits only as little John Bulls is to attribute to Tolkien a provincialism which he does not in fact have. The hobbit character could be expressed in any national literature; their humanness, such as it is, reflects mankind in general rather than Englishmen in particular.

Hobbits are, as Professor Miller has said, easy for the reader to identify with. This is felt by people who would never put it in critical terms like "identify." Try this experiment sometime: go around putting up posters for a Tolkien Society meeting. Someone will come up and ask you, 'What's that?' You say it's for people who like Tolkien's stories. He asks what are they about? Then, try one of two things. You can say, 'They're about elves and battles and dragons!' And he will say, 'Gmnhmnmf', and walk away. Or you can say, 'They're about some people who like beer and don't want to get involved in adventures'. And he will say, 'Where's the meeting? Can other people come?'

Hobbits, in other words, are the aspect of humanity which I have dubbed, for the purposes of this paper, Everyclod—unjustly, of course. For as we all know, "there is more to them than meets the eye."

Tolkien has done his portraiture finely. We are all in some way small, provincial, and comfort-loving—and we see ourselves as such. At first we like to imagine ourselves as heroes, but experience makes us sceptical; we become convinced that, in fairness, we are not heroes. Maybe as Lords of the Jungle we broke the neighbor's shadetree, and got spanked. Maybe our term in the army ended, but the war kept on for years. Maybe 'our' leading man married another leading lady. We become wary of admitting even to ourselves that we like to see ourselves as heroic. One of the notable features of twentieth-century literature is the antihero; Northrop Frye's ironic literary mode has taken over our everyday lives. Everyclod is at the center of our vision, which has become cloddish.

But this is not Tolkien's mode. One of the reasons he is likable and unusual among contemporary authors is that he does not focus on the cloddish, though he does focus on hobbits. Bilbo, Frodo, Sam, Merry, and Pippin are all to a greater or

lesser extent billed as Everyclod at the beginnings of their stories, but as we know, each of them becomes a hero. Bilbo, who
"looks more like a grocer than a burglar" (*The Hobbit*, p. 30),
becomes brave in direct combat with the Mirkwood spiders and
resourceful in indirect combat when he elicits the knowledge of
Smaug's soft spot. It is not strictly accurate to say, as I just did,
that Bilbo becomes brave, or Sam heroic, or Frodo holy. The
seeds of these qualities were in them to begin with, and the circumstances of their adventures allow the qualities to emerge
like a developing photograph. With the hobbits, what Tolkien
shows us is that, and how, Everyclod really is Everyhero, and
can develop his heroic nature when the need arises.

Hobbits, then, are Tolkien's primary picture of Man. But
then, what of the characters he portrays as men, members of the
human race? He has already embodied some human aspects in
other races; for instance, instead of having a man who is a miner
or a smith, who prefers stone buildings with ornaments of met-
alwork, Tolkien uses a dwarf. C.S. Lewis points this out: "Much
that in realistic work would be done by 'character delineation'
is here done simply by making the character an elf, a dwarf or
a hobbit. The imagined beings have their insides on the outside;
they are visible souls."[4] In this case, we may ask what aspect of
man is portrayed by the characters who are human? Since
Tolkien has given himself the option of making his characters
human or otherwise, he must mean something by making them
so. What are his men like?

Tolkien's human race, in the specimens we encounter, has
much more variety than any of the other races. From petty vil-
lains like Bill Ferny, through the loathsome Grima, to that portrait of damnation, poor Denethor; from the slow-thinking
Butterbur, through the martial Eomer to the king, Aragorn. Not
to mention the gentle warrior Faramir, the hero-villain Boromir,
the resurrected epic Théoden and the warrior-maid Éowyn (a
fascinating character). The first thing to be said of the human
race, in Tolkien's portrait, is that it is capable of any act: treachery, warcraft, gentleness, domesticity, adventurousness, or
poetry. And this leaves us where we were before: hobbits are
Tolkien's basic kind of people, and the human race is too various to abstract a composite picture from its members and say,
This is Tolkien's man.

In that case, look again. What if, instead of seeking a composite picture, we look for a representative? Can we say that in all this variety of men, there is one man *par excellence*? Of course we can. Obviously, Tolkien's man *par excellence* is Aragorn. So let us consider him and see what he adds to Tolkien's picture of humanity. So far, we have the image of Everyclod with Everyhero sleeping inside him. Aragorn is a hero already, and what sleeps in him is kingship.

Aragorn appears in a number of guises, and all of them are quite the opposite of things hobbitish. Aragorn is not small, either in body or in mind: men are bigger than hobbits, and Strider is a tall man. He is not provincial. In fact, we learn fairly early that the Rangers (whose chief he is) have been protecting the Shire's borders within which the hobbits have become so provincial. The Rangers are aware of the major issues, the beauty and the evil outside the Shire of which the typical hobbit has no conception whatever. Aragorn is also not particularly comfort-loving. One supposes that, as is true for all of Tolkien's characters, he appreciates the amenities when he can get them. Indeed, we first see him (I, p. 214) with a tankard and a pipe. But we also see mud on his boots and travel stains on his cloak, and he himself is "weather-beaten," implying that his usual abode (though not his rightful abode) is less comfortable than a hobbit hole.

So Tolkien's man *par excellence* is very different from his race *par excellence*. Aragorn must, so to speak, 'refer' to a different aspect of humanity from the hobbits, who (as we have seen) refer to Everyclod, the individual who has heroic potential.

I must apologize briefly for saying Aragorn "is about" or "refers" to something. Really, of course, Aragorn is Aragorn (Strider, Elessar, Estel, Thorongil), the Dúnadan, the man in Tolkien's story.

But, what is Aragorn about? What other aspect of man is so important? There is his bad side, but Strider does not represent that, despite the mixed impressions created by his first appearance. Evils are amply covered by orcs, Saruman, Ted Sandyman, and so on. Nor does Aragorn represent our Everyclod aspect, even with its latent heroism, for his heroism is not latent. He is a heroic hero, the sort we feel shy of identifying ourselves with. He is a hero, and more than that, the king: the epitome of his race, and in that sense its representative.

But look at the condition this king is in throughout most of the story: he is not in his rightful place, and he is surrounded by symbols of a realm not in its rightful order. The throne is vacant. A steward governs in the city of Gondor, whose name is no longer the Tower of the Setting Sun but the Tower of Guard. In the city houses stand empty. The White Tree is withered. The sword Narsil is broken. Aragorn is the king's heir, but he is in exile from his realm. He is engaged to Arwen, but they are not married. In fact, the first time we see her, at a feast, he is closeted in council elsewhere.

By the conclusion of the story, these conditions are all set right: Narsil is reforged as Anduril; a seedling of the Tree is found; the city is on its way to being rebuilt and repopulated; Aragorn and Arwen are married and reigning. This is Tolkien's fortunate resolution, or if you will, happy ending.

Do we know anyone else who is out of his rightful position, whose restoration would be a fortunate event? Yes, we do. It is not you or me or him or her (Farmer Maggot, or Rosie Cotton); it is *us*.

Now I shall refer to Christian doctrine, which we have inherited in the form of Judeo-Christian myth. Tolkien is a Christian himself, and a look at this body of beliefs throws light on his story at this point. The rightful position of man is to be the ruling creature on this planet, to administer it in the best interests of all the local creatures, and God's viceroy. As you know, man now occupies only a parody of this position: he is the ruling creature here, but he kills his own kind and other creatures and damages and exploits the planet.

In the history of mankind, there are two men *par excellence* whom it behooves us to consider while talking of Aragorn: Adam, and Christ, who is called the new Adam.

Adam was set at his creation into the kingly position I have described. And he failed. And all his descendants after him have been dislocated from our place on earth. Adam (and in him all mankind) is parallel to Aragorn in that both are exiles. But Aragorn does not fail. He bides his time, works, follows his opportunities, resists temptations, and brings all the realm to good. Notice that he can only do this in co-operation with Everyclod—in fact, with all good creatures.

Tom Bombadil, by the way, has been called "the unfallen Adam."[5] This is a perceptive appellation. I don't mean that

Tolkien said to himself, 'Now I will put in a prelapsarian'; but surely Adam in Eden must have been similar in many way to Tom as described: the master of all natural things, but not their owner (I, p. 174). But Adam fell, and his race's predicament follows from that. Tom is a survivor from another age, and peripheral to the War of the Ring, while the king in exile is central to it.

Christ is the true good event. He came, an actual person, in time and space, to repair for us the breach which Adam had made. Christ repairs the relationship between mankind and the extraterrestrial Creator. He does not repair the politics, economics, or ecology of the planet Earth. As He plainly said, "My kingdom is not of this world."

But Aragorn's kingdom *is* of this world. He is born to reign in Middle-earth. Aragorn is parallel to Christ only in that each of them is the man of good events in his story, not in the kind of fortunate conclusion they bring. True, they have some manifestations in common: most noticeably, each can heal the sick and each is crowded upon by the sick in consequence. I do not think one need make much to-do about a Biblical parallel, on the crowding: it is only a piece of realism. If there is a healer, he will be pestered; think of the proverbial doctor at the cocktail party.

Aragorn's good work, then, is that of the restoration of the king on earth. And this is a type, a figure, a symbol, of the happy turnabout of the restoration of man as a race. Individually, we are hobbits; collectively, we are Aragorn.

NOTES TO CHAPTER 5

1. David Miller, 'Hobbits: Common Lens for Heroic Experience', *Tolkien Journal, XI-Orcrist* 3 (1969), pp. 11–15.

2. J.R.R. Tolkien, *The Lord of the Rings* (New York: Ballantine Books, 1965) All references in this chapter are to this edition.

3. J.R.R. Tolkien, *The Hobbit:Or, There and Back Again* (New York: Ballantine Books, 1965). All references are to this edition.

4. C.S. Lewis, 'The Dethronement of Power'. Reprinted in Neil D. Isaacs and Rose A. Zimbardo, *Tolkien and the Critics* (South Bend: Notre Dame University Press, 1968), p. 15.

5. Alexis Levitin, 'The Hero in J.R.R. Tolkien's *The Lord of the Rings*', *Mankato State College Studies in English*, II, 1 (February, 1967), p. 32.

6

The Interlace Structure of
The Lord of the Rings

RICHARD C. WEST

One of the early reviews of *The Lord of the Rings* called it "perhaps the last literary masterpiece of the Middle Ages."[1] There is more wit than justice in the comment, for the book is addressed to the modern world and is esteemed by a great many readers who are not medieval scholars. Lover of the past though he certainly is, J.R.R. Tolkien was nonetheless our contemporary. Moreover, any medieval author would, in passing on a tradition of long standing, have dressed it in the fashion of his day. Paradoxically, Tolkien would not be 'medieval' unless he 'modernized' his work. Nevertheless, there is some truth in the observation, and good reason for the tendency of critics of *The Lord of the Rings* to grope among old epics, romances, and sagas for analogues to Tolkien's achievement.[2] What I would like to do in this chapter is attempt to extract from earlier literature some light to shed on the form of *The Lord of the Rings*.

It was, I believe, George H. Thomson who first pointed out that to produce "a detailed yet panoramic view of a whole world in movement and turmoil,"[3] Tolkien used a structural technique similar to that of medieval interlace. This was a narrative mode of such complexity and sophistication that, until recently, modern critics could not detect a coherent design in most medieval romances. Over two hundred years ago Bishop Hurd observed that Spenser's works and their 'Gothic' models were "intertwining . . . several actions together, in order to give something like the appearance of one action,"[4] but it was not investigated seriously until early in this century when the French historian, Ferdinand Lot, described what he called *entrelacement* in the *Prose Lancelot*.[5] Building on Lot's work, Eugène Vinaver significantly refined the 'interlace' technique,[6] and other scholars have made worthwhile contributions.[7]

The nature of the interlace technique becomes clearer by contrasting it with the modern structural technique of 'organic unity' with which we are more familiar. Organic unity seeks to reduce the chaotic flux of reality to manageable terms by imposing a clear and fairly simple pattern upon it. It calls for a progressive and uncluttered narrative line in which there is a single major theme to which a limited number of other themes may be related so long as they are kept subordinate. The main theme grows from a clear-cut beginning through a middle which develops naturally ('organically') from the beginning to a resolution which is the product of all that preceded it. It is considered preferable to have a limited number of characters and to have no more than one or two dominate the action. Any single work should be self-sufficient, containing within itself everything that is necessary to it and excluding everything that is not necessary. In other words, the organic work is indivisible in itself but divided from everything else. The principles of organic unity are summed up in the dictum of the Queen of Hearts: begin at the beginning and go on till you come to the end; then stop.

Interlace, by contrast, seeks to mirror the perception of the flux of events in the world around us, where everything is happening at once. Its narrative line is digressive and cluttered, dividing our attention among an indefinite number of events, characters, and themes, any one of which may dominate at any given time, and it is often indifferent to cause and effect relationships. The paths of the characters cross, diverge, and recross, and the story passes from one to another and then another but does not follow a single line. Also, the narrator implies that there are innumerable events that he has not had time to tell us about; moreover, no attempt is made to provide a clear-cut beginning or end to the story. We feel that we have interrupted the chaotic activity of the world at a certain point and followed a selection from it for a time, and that after we leave, it continues on its own random path. The author, or someone else, may perhaps take up the threads of the story again later and add to it at beginning, middle, or end.

Yet the apparently casual form of the interlace is deceptive; it actually has a very subtle kind of cohesion. No part of the narrative can be removed without damage to the whole, for within any given section there are echoes of previous parts and anticipations of later ones. The medieval memory (lacking modern information retrieval systems and therefore necessarily greater than ours) delighted in following repetitions and variations of themes, whether their different appearances were separated by scores or hundreds of pages. Musical art gives an analogous aesthetic pleasure and shows a similar structural binding (I think this is why C.S. Lewis called Spenser's interlace "polyphonic narrative"), but in literature, the interlace structure also allows detailed examination of any number of facets of a theme.

Moreover, though events are in flux there is a pattern underlying them. In the Old French *Queste del Saint Graal* we pursue not only the Holy Grail but the ideals of knighthood through the adventures of Gawain, Bors, Lancelot, Galahad, and others, our response to any one adventure being molded to a large extent by comparison or contrast of that adventure with the others. But we do not limit ourselves to any single meaning for any happening: while 'unified'"narrative generally isolates a single cause of an event to achieve a frequently powerful and intense effect, interlaced narrative usually assigns numerous causes for any event thereby reflecting the complex interrelatedness we actually see in life. We are accustomed to an illusion of reality provided by adherence to the possible or the plausible. Medieval authors loved to seize on fantastic elements (magicians, monsters, and the like) for entertaining digressions, yet the people and events of the imaginary world take on depth and solidity because of their detail and mutual interaction.

Direct Medieval Influence Is Doubtful

Interlace reached the peak of its development in the French cyclic romances of the thirteenth century, but variations of the form can be found at least as early as the Roman poet Ovid's *Metamorphoses* and at least as late as Spenser's *Faerie Queene*. It is easy to see how the form could become bewilderingly complex, and the preference in the later Middle Ages for shorter narrative units indicates that authors and audiences came to desire briefer and clearer stories. Out of this movement toward single-ness came the modern novel, which remained for the most part associated with the structural techniques of organic unity until recently, when writers like James Joyce, Marcel Proust, Günter Grass, and William Faulkner once again began experimenting with varieties of the interlace.

Different as he was from such authors in most respects, Professor Tolkien was like them both in sharing in the move-ment of Western letters away from 'realism' in the direction of 'fantasy' and in his use of interlace. It is possible, though I have my doubts, that in *The Lord of the Rings* we have an example of direct influence by the medieval form on a mod-ern work of art.[8] Professor Tolkien said himself that his medieval studies fertilized his imagination, that his typical response upon reading a medieval work was to desire not so much to make a philological or critical study of it as to write a modern work in the same tradition.[9] Thus he wrote a sequel to *The Battle of Maldon,* a verse play in the alliterative meter of the Old English poem.[10] A number of poems in the same early medieval meter appear in *The Lord of the Rings,* and a poem addressed to W.H. Auden[11] is actually written in Old English formulas. The opening lines of 'The Lay of Aotrou and Itroun'[12] claim their inspiration from the Breton lay tradition. *Farmer Giles of Ham* parodies various medieval genres.[13] 'Imram'[14] recounts the fabulous voyage of St. Brendan. Bonniejean Christensen has discerned connections between *Beowulf* and *The Hobbit,*[15] and George H. Thomson has pointed out how important traditional romance themes are in *The Lord of the Rings.*[16]

I repeat that I find this influence dubious. Tolkien was known not to be fond of the French language or its literature, and I doubt that he would have been so impressed by an Old French form that he would have deliberately borrowed it. I think it is more likely that the psychic affinity a scholar often devel-ops for his period of study influences his total outlook. Tolkien's sympathy would naturally lie with medieval romance structure. He may simply have reinvented the interlace to accommodate the story he had to tell: the nature of his material requires just such a form.

The Six Books of *The Lord of the Rings*

The story is fundamentally a simple one: the quest of the hobbit, Frodo Baggins, to take the One Ring of Power to the place of its forging at Mount Orodruin, where alone it can be unmade, and destroy it and the threat of its power and corruption. But in the land of Middle-earth this quest naturally lies interwoven into the lives and fates of other persons and peoples. The quest theme is primary, but another major theme is the war against Sauron, who seeks to dominate Middle-earth and would be victorious if he could recover the ruling Ring he lost in an ancient war. For their different reasons, all peoples are drawn into the struggle, on one side or the other. Tolkien's main story thus involves many other stories, all more or less independent yet linked at many points and occurring more or less simultaneously.

We may first describe the overall structure of *The Lord of the Rings*. "Of course, the present division into Volumes," writes Tolkien, "mere practical necessity of publication, is a falsification. As is shown by the unsatisfactory titles of the last two Volumes. The work is in no legitimate literary sense a 'trilogy.' It is a three-decker novel. The only units of any structural significance are the 'books.' These originally had each its title. Personally I should have preferred that this arrangement should have been preserved with the volumes designated merely by numbers . . ."[17] If we restore those titles,[18] we see that they underline the two major themes of the quest and the war.

As George H. Thomson notes, Tolkien permits himself a certain neatness of plot at beginning and end, while reserving the most complex interweaving for the central portion.[19] Book I, 'The First Journey', builds up the main theme: Frodo and his hobbit friends Merry, Pippin, and Sam leave the peaceful Shire on the first stages of the quest. The four hobbits are caught up in the turbulent events of the world beyond their borders, and through many dangers they bear the ring to Rivendell, where plans are made for its destruction. They set out almost in a holiday spirit, but mystery and peril begin to strip them of their complacency and innocence, test their mettle, and prepare them for the later stages of the quest. In Book II, 'The Journey of the Nine Companions', the quest theme is continued, enriched with retrospective material concerning the history of the ring (its

making, its power, its loss, its finding by Bilbo) and a fellowship
in which all the Free Peoples of Middle-earth are represented is
formed to carry out the task of unmaking the ring. But the fellowship is fragmented at the end of Book II, in part by internal
dissensions which divide Sauron's enemies. Frodo leaves,
accompanied by his inseparable servant, Sam, and is pursued by
Gollum. Book IV, 'The Journey of the Ring-bearers', and the
early part of Book VI, 'The End of the Third Age', recount their
adventures as they creep pathetically across the desolation of
Mordor. Meanwhile the rest of Middle-earth clashes in war that
will be decided by the success or failure of the quest. The other
members of the Fellowship become entangled in the wars of
Rohan and Gondor and are parted and reunited many times in
Books III and V. Parallel plot lines in Book III, 'The Treason of
Isengard', are Gandalf's awakening of the Rohirrim, and Merry's
and Pippin's awakening of the ents to the menace of Isengard,
an imitation Mordor. In Book V, 'The War of the Ring'," Merry
swears fealty to Théoden, king of Rohan, while Pippin enters
the service of Denethor, steward of Gondor. Aragorn is a mighty
warrior, so much of the fighting naturally devolves upon him,
and he moves about to be present at virtually every major battle. Gandalf, like Merlin the wise counselor of kings in time of
crisis, becomes the chief strategist of the war. The themes are
resolved in the latter part of Book VI, 'The End of the Third
Age', as the friends come together again before each turning to
set his home in order.[20]

Echoes and Anticipations

Even a reader unconcerned with literary form or structure must
notice, at least unconsciously, the apparently meandering manner of the plot. The meeting with the ents in Book III will serve
as an illustration. As actors in the narrative, the ents serve to
overthrow the wizard Saruman, a traitor who desires the ring for
himself and has set up a citadel modeled on Sauron's. Thus they
eliminate the powerful foe of the men of Rohan and enable
them to help the men of Gondor in the war against Sauron. But
the ents march against Saruman in the first place not merely
because of his hostile actions against them, but because they
have learned his intentions from Merry and Pippin. The hobbits
would never have met the ents if they had not been captured

by orcs and brought to the area of Fangorn Forest, where the orcs were destroyed by a party of Rohirrim (who were acting without royal authority, a circumstance which causes complications later in the story). The orcs, ironically, had intended to bring the hobbits to Saruman, and the episode illustrates an evil action recoiling on the doer, something that happens often in *The Lord of the Rings*. It was not only Saruman's orcs who were involved in the attack on the fellowship, but also another band in the service of Sauron who wanted to avenge the death of one of their chieftains in the running battle fought as the company passed through their territory in Moria. The Fellowship was going through Moria because . . . and so on—thus the chain of events can be traced as far back in the history of the Ring as the reader pleases. Such casual collisions of disparate people and events—in a manner familiar because it is the way in which things seem to us to happen in our own lives—knit the fabric of the story. The ents are hardly creatures who wait in the wings to be called on to attack Saruman; rather as Treebeard tells the hobbits, "I go my own way; but your way may go along with mine for a while!"[21] These tree-herds have their own story, but it has points of contact with the war and the quest. Removing them from the narrative would destroy the cohesiveness of the whole. The narrative is not loose, except to a superficial view; everything is interconnected.

Indeed, as with medieval interlace, Tolkien's narrative creates an infinite series of echoes and anticipations by which the work gains coherence. The numerous prophecies in the story are invariably validated sooner or later. The grisly detail of Isildur cutting the Ring of Power from the hand of Sauron (I, p. 319) is repeated as Gollum bites off Frodo's ring-finger and is borne into the fire by the weight of the Ring (III, pp. 275–76). The lost finger thus becomes a symbol of imperfection and evil and makes Frodo's decision to keep the ring for himself a decision to become another Sauron. When Treebeard asks Pippin and Merry if they have seen any of the entwives in the Shire, our sense of the poignancy of their negative response will be increased if we remember the conversation (hundreds of pages back) in the Green Dragon inn, where we heard that giant tree-like beings have indeed been seen walking in the Shire (I, p. 73). Tolkien, like Marlowe and Milton before him, can use proper names for their sheer musical beauty, but he uses them also to gain a sense of the legendary past—the mortal Beren's love for the elf-maiden Lúthien Tinúviel parallels the romance of Aragorn and Arwen; Gil-galad and Elendil who led the Last Alliance of Elves and Men against Sauron; Celebrimbor who forged the Three Rings, Eärendil the mariner (especially his star, which now and then shines hope into the enemies of Sauron, as when Sam looks on it from Mordor); the dwarf-lord Durin, and places such as Númenor, Nargothrond, and Gondolin. We may be traveling through faery lands forlorn, peopled by imaginary beings, but the history, geography, and cultures of each cross one another with such complexity that we have the impression that the fantasy has lifelike depth and solidity.

The story of Shelob in Book IV is an example of interwoven themes. This is an exciting, memorable episode, yet it cannot be treated as a complete episode. Frodo and Sam only come to Shelob's lair because the movements of Sauron's armies in the War of the Ring have closed the other entrances to Mordor. This provides another example of evil action recoiling on the doer. Gollum has hoped to use Shelob to destroy the hobbits, but ironically, he furthers the quest by guiding the ring bearers, who could not have found their own way into the Black Land. Shelob represents an ancient evil independent of Sauron's (in the interlaced narrative, there are many antagonists, just as there are many protagonists), and, like other evil beings in this romance, she is associated with blackness, darkness, and filth. The flashing starglass with which the hobbits drive away Shelob is related to the archetypical images of light and darkness which recur throughout the work. That phial of light is a gift of the elf queen, Galadriel, and recalls the sojourn of the Fellowship in the Golden Wood of Lórien. When Frodo is stung by Shelob's paralyzing poison and apparently succumbs to the darkness of death (as was prophetically foreshadowed in the Mirror of Galadriel), Sam heroically though reluctantly, assumes responsibility for the quest. Sam's dilemma—that he must leave his master though he is inseparable from him—has been a motif all along: he has come with him from the Shire (I, p. 98), watched by him while he was recovering from the wound inflicted by the ringwraith (I, p. 292), followed him uninvited to the secret Council of Elrond (I, p. 355) and was the only one to go with Frodo when he left the rest of the fellowship (I, p. 526). When Faramir awakens Frodo and leads him to look through the

Window on the West, Sam, as if invisibly bound to his master, instantly wakes and follows them (II, p. 370). So it is part of the pattern that Sam will be reunited with Frodo and go on to give essential help in the achievement of the quest by getting Frodo to the fire and then by getting him away from it. Shelob meanwhile retreats into her dark lair and out of the story: that her brief appearance has been so significant is in part the result of its resonance with themes running all through the book.

Since, in the interlace pattern, any one section of a work implies other sections both earlier and later, any attempt to enumerate the interwoven threads of the narrative will end in giving a résumé of the entire book. But I will examine one additional section to reinforce my analysis.

Dreams and Nightmares

Early in Book I, the four hobbits spend the night in the house of Tom Bombadil, the master of wood and hill. Here, say Tom and his wife, Goldberry, no evil influence can affect them. And we are told the dreams of three of the hobbits.

> In the dead night, Frodo lay in a dream without light. Then he saw the young moon rising; under its thin light there loomed before him a black wall of rock, pierced by a dark arch like a great gate. It seemed to Frodo that he was lifted up, and passing over he saw that the rock-wall was a circle of hills, and that within it was a plain, and in the midst of the plain stood a pinnacle of stone, like a vast tower but not made by hands. On its top stood the figure of a man. The moon as it rose seemed to hang for a moment above his head and glistened in his white hair as the wind stirred it. Up from the dark plain below came the crying of fell voices, and the howling of many wolves. Suddenly a shadow, like the shape of great wings, passed across the moon. The figure lifted his arms and a light flashed from the staff that he wielded. A mighty eagle swept down and bore him away. The voices wailed and the wolves yammered. There was a noise like a strong wind blowing, and on it was borne the sound of hoofs, galloping, galloping, galloping from the East. "Black Riders!" thought Frodo as he wakened, with the sound of the hoofs still echoing in his mind. He wondered if he would ever again have the courage to leave the safety of these stone walls. He lay motionless, still listening; but all was now silent, and at last he turned and fell asleep again or wandered into some other unremembered dream. (I, p. 177)

Frodo's dream may seem meaningless at this point, but not if we read further. At the Council of Elrond in Book II it develops that he has had a vision of Gandalf, the wizard of fire and light,[22] attracting the attention of Gwaihir, the chief of the eagles of the Misty Mountains, in order to be rescued from the pinnacle of Orthanc where he was being held prisoner by Saruman. This had in fact already occurred, and though Frodo associates the hoof-beats with the pursuing ringwraiths, it is more likely that they belong to Shadowfax, who was even then bearing Gandalf toward the shire (III, p. 464). Ill dreams tormented Frodo during his last days in Hobbiton, but this dream has greater significance and is wound more tightly into the narrative than they are. Frodo has found Bombadil's house to be another idyllic retreat, one which seems more likely than the Shire to remain permanently safe; when he does find the courage to continue the quest despite this warning, the theme of personal responsibility is heightened by his decision to carry out his original intention. Also, this dream gives us our first sight of Saruman's hill-walled citadel, and the image will remain in our minds when we learn of the mountain-walled citadel of Mordor of which Saruman's powerful stronghold is only a copy. The wall becomes an image of the might of evil and works its effect on the imagination of the reader—this dark, stone-barriered place from which an evil power can issue and in which it seems unassailable disheartens the characters in the book and similarly disheartens us.

Moreover, Frodo's dream also marks the first appearance in *The Lord of the Rings* of the eagle motif, later repeated. Several times at the end of the first volume and the beginning of the second, Legolas, Gimli, and Aragorn spot a distant shape in the sky and wonder what it is and what its errand is.

When they are finally reunited with Gandalf, they learn that this was Gwaihir, who had again rescued the wizard (this time from the peak of Mount Zirak-Zigil where he lay after his fateful encounter with the Balrog of Moria) and carried him to the elves in Lothlórien. It was by Gandalf that the eagle had been sent to watch river and field. The eagle motif is then dropped until the third volume when in the battle before Mordor at the end of Book V Pippin hears a cry:

"The Eagles are coming! The Eagles are coming!" For one moment more Pippin's thought hovered. "Bilbo!" it said. "But no! That came in his tale, long long ago. This is my tale, and it is ended now. Goodbye!" And his thought fled far away and his eyes saw no more. (III, p. 208)

This sends us back to the parallel situation in *The Hobbit*, when Bilbo, also just before losing consciousness, shouted the same cry, signifying the nearly decisive entry of the eagles into the battle of Five Armies.[23] By the end of the book this image will become a symbol of hope and of a higher power bringing unexpected help in time of need. We will have been prepared for their rescue from the destruction of Mordor: "and down swept Gwaihir, and down came Landroval and Meneldor the swift; and in a dream, not knowing what fate had befallen them, the wanderers were lifted up and borne far away out of the darkness and the fire" (III, p. 282).

Let us now turn back to Pippin and Merry, asleep in the house of Tom Bombadil. Their dreams will require less comment:

Pippin lay dreaming pleasantly; but a change came over his dreams and he turned and groaned. Suddenly he woke, or thought he had waked, and yet still heard in the darkness the sound that had disturbed his dream: *tip-tap, squeak:* the noise was like branches fretting in the wind, twig-fingers scraping wall and window: *creak, creak, creak.* He wondered if there were willow-trees close to the house; and then suddenly he had a dreadful feeling that he was not in an ordinary house at all, but inside the willow and listening to that horrible dry creaking voice laughing at him again. He sat up, and felt the soft pillows yield to his hands, and he lay down again relieved. He seemed to hear the echo of words in his ears: "Fear nothing! Have peace until the morning! Heed no nightly noises!" Then he went to sleep again. . . .

It was the sound of water that Merry heard falling into his quiet sleep: water streaming down gently, and then spreading, spreading irresistibly all round the house into a dark shoreless pool. It gurgled under the walls, and was rising slowly but surely. "I shall be drowned!" he thought. "It will find its way in, and then I shall drown." He felt that he was lying in a soft slimy bog, and springing up he set his foot on the corner of a cold hard flagstone. Then he remembered where he was and lay down again. He seemed to hear or remember hearing: "Nothing passes doors or windows save moonlight and starlight and the wind off the hill-top." A little breath of sweet air moved the curtain. He breathed deep and fell asleep again. (I, pp. 177–78)

The nightmares that Pippin and Merry experience are unlike Frodo's visionary dream,[24] but they are similar to each other in tone and in circumstance, each being soothed by the enchanted singing of Tom Bombadil. Like any other natural force, Tom is neutral toward others. ("Tom has his house to mind and Goldberry is waiting"); nevertheless, he is naturally benevolent to those who do cross his path, that being the nature of the paradisal state of which he is a survivor.[25] The two dreams are different in their focus, Pippin's looking backward and Merry's forward in time, but they concern similar matters. Pippin recalls the hobbits' plight when they were seized by the ancient evil willow, from which Bombadil had rescued them (I, p. 169). Merry's dream recurs a few chapters later, while he lies on the ground in a faint, overcome by the evil influence of a Ringwraith (I, pp. 235–36).

Purpose Behind Chance Events

Thus the technique of interlace can mirror the ebb and flow of events; it may also show purpose or pattern behind change. Tolkien has emphasized this by a motif threaded throughout the work. Gandalf says cryptically that Bilbo was *meant* to find the ring by someone other than its maker and that Frodo also was *meant* to have it (I, p. 88). Gildor and a company of elves frighten away a Black Rider who was close on the trail of the hobbits, and Gildor says there may be more than chance in their meeting (I, p. 124). Tom Bombadil was returning home from an errand of his own when he came upon the hobbits who had been caught by Old Man Willow: "Just chance brought me then," he says, "if chance you call it" (I, p. 175). The various leaders of men, elves, and dwarves who participate in the Council of Elrond all came to Rivendell for their own reasons and were not summoned by Elrond Half-Elven; yet he tells them that they have been called to find counsel for the peril of the world (I, p. 318). Frodo comes to realize that he has been appointed, as Bilbo's heir to the ring, to carry on the quest to destroy the ring because he is an innocent hobbit without the power to make full use of the One Ring and can resist its temptation and corrupting influence better than any of the Wise and the Great (Gandalf, Elrond, Galadriel, and Faramir all refuse it for this reason). But who or by whom appointed he cannot say. Gandalf and Frodo sense that Gollum's fate is tied to the ring, and their belief is justified by the conclusion of the quest. Examples could easily be multiplied. Events are not governed deterministically, for everyone seems to himself to be acting freely and has good reasons for his actions. However, the underlying pattern is there.

Another cohesive element is the image of the shadow which reappears throughout the narrative. We begin in the idyllic and bucolic shire at the edge of the shadow and progress through darker and darker lands to the ultimate peril of Mordor, which actually lies under a shadow. The overthrow of Sauron lifts the shadow. This pattern is reflected stylistically, moreover, as the homely middle-class British speech of the hobbits is gradually replaced by the more elegant diction of a heroic age. The title of the first chapter, 'A Long-Expected Party', recalls the title of the opening chapter of *The Hobbit,* 'An Unexpected Party', suggesting both relation and difference; also, the fairy tale opening of 'Bilbo Baggins was eleven-one years old' shades into the epic finale.

It is not uncommon for a critical essay to reflect its subject: this paper is itself somewhat interlaced, and the various structural facets singled out and discussed are all interconnected. What I have said may be considered suggestive rather than exhaustive, and it would be easy to find other illustrations of interlace in *The Lord of the Rings:* no single protagonist but a great many individual stories that cross one another; coherence among the interwoven stories; the appearance of a pattern behind the flux of events; recurring themes and motifs providing aesthetic and intellectual satisfaction; the events of an imaginary world gaining the illusion of depth and solidity by their mutual interaction and weight of detail.

Let me end by citing one other characteristic of the interlace—the effect of what might be called open-endedness, whereby the reader has the impression that the story has an existence outside the confines of the book and that the author could have begun earlier or ended later, if he had chosen. Since Tolkien's romance is a section only (however large) of a vast mythology, it is just such an effect he wants. Hence the appendices are a necessary adjunct, for they give us information about the earlier history of Middle-earth, happenings elsewhere at the time of the story that are not recounted in the text proper, and what happened to the principal characters after the point at which the romance stops. This effect of open-endedness has been well described in the conversation of Sam and Frodo, resting on the stairs of Cirith Ungol as they cross the mountains into Mordor:

> "Beren now, he never thought he was going to get that Silmaril from the Iron Crown in Thangorodrim, and yet he did, and that was worse place and a blacker danger than ours. But that's a long tale, of course, and goes on past the happiness and into grief and beyond it—and the Silmaril went on and came to Earendil. And why, sir, I never thought of that before! We've got—you've got some of the light of it in that star-glass that the Lady gave you! Why, to think of it, we're in the same tale still! Don't the great tales never end?"
>
> "No, they never end as tales," said Frodo. "But the people in them come, and go when their part's ended. Our part will end later—or sooner." (III, p. 408).

Real life goes on indefinitely; a work of literature is different from actual living and must end somewhere, but the finality is arbitrary and the resolution artificial—which is, in part, the strength of the interlace. *The Lord of the Rings* is not the last literary masterpiece of the Middle Ages, but it was, if nothing more, a just instinct that led Tolkien to choose a medieval technique for his modern masterpiece.[26]

NOTES TO CHAPTER 6

1. William Blissett, 'Despots of the Rings', *South Atlantic Quarterly* 58 (Summer 1959), p. 449.

2. The use of the imaginary *Red Book of Westmarch* is an example of a medieval tradition adapted for a modern audience. From the point of view of medieval aesthetics, originality was not a virtue but a defect: the new had not yet proven its worth, whereas the old had stood the test of time. A medieval author saw his task as that of handing on old matter in a worthy fashion, and if he altered it in the process he was quite likely to pretend that he had a learned source authorizing the change. Tolkien's *Red Book*, pastiche of scholarship though it is, functions as such a medieval 'spurious source', but the 'authority' it imparts is by an appeal not to the tried-and-true but to the modern mystique of 'scholarly research'.

3. '*The Lord of the Rings:* The Novel as Traditional Romance', *Wisconsin Studies in Comtemporary Literature* 8 (Winter, 1967), p. 49. This excellent article first suggested the approach of this chapter to me.

4. Bishop Richard Hurd, in the eighth of his *Letters on Chivalry and Romance* (1762). My quotation is taken from the edition by Edith J. Morley (London: Henry Frawde, 1911), p. 123.

5. *Étude sur le Lancelot en prose* (Paris, 1918). The *Prose Lancelot* is a lengthy romance, the main portion of the Arthurian Vulgate Cycle, dating from early in the thirteenth century.

6. See especially 'The Poetry of Interlace', Chapter 5 (pp. 68–98) of his *The Rise of Romance* (New York: Oxford University Press, 1971). See also: *Form and Meaning in Medieval Romance* (Modern Humanities Research Association, 1966); the preface and notes in his three-volume edition of *The Works of Sir Thomas Malory* (Oxford University Press, first edition 1947; second edition 1967); and 'Morgue la fée et le principe de l'entrelacement', *Bulletin Bibliographique de la Société Internationale Arthurienne* 18 (Paris, 1966), p. 168.

7. Rosemund Tuve, *Allegorical Imagery: Some Medieval Books and Their Posterity* (Princeton: Princeton University Press, 1966), especially Chapter 5, 'Romances' (pp. 335–436); C.S. Lewis, 'Edmund Spenser, 1552–99', in his *Studies in Medieval and Renaissance Literature*, edited by Walter Hooper (Cambridge: Cambridge University Press, 1966), pp. 121–145; John Legerle, 'The Interlace Structure of *Beowulf*', *University of Toronto Quarterly* 37 (1967), pp. 1–17; A.P. Campbell, 'The Time Element of Interlace Structure in *Beowulf*, *Neuphilologische Mitteilungen* 70 (1969), pp. 425–435; Gwyn Jones, *Kings, Beasts, and Heroes,* (New York: Oxford University Press, 1972), pp. 28–33. Jones discusses the parallels within *Beowulf* but is skeptical that interlace has a large role in the structure of the poem. The echoes and foreshadowings detectable in *Beowulf* still leave us, he says, "a long way short of postulating a theory of Old English poetical composition analogous with the interlace designs common in Anglo-Saxon visual art" (pp. 31–32).

8. It is perhaps worth noting, in this connection, that both Joyce and Proust were also interested in medieval literature.

9. A remark made to an audience at Oxford who had come to hear Tolkien lecture on philology and instead heard him recite a poem of his own composition. I am indebted to Professor Eugene Vinaver for this information.

10. 'The Homecoming of Beorhtnoth Beorhthelm's Son', *Essays and Studies of the English Association*, New Series, 6 (1953), pp. 1–18. Reprinted in *The Tolkien Reader* (New York: Ballantine, 1966).

11. 'For W.H.A.' *Shenandoah* 18 (Winter, 1967), pp. 96–97.

12. *Welsh Review* 4 (December, 1945), pp. 254–266.

13. See J.A. Johnston, '*Farmer Giles of Ham:* What Is It?' *Orcrist* 7 (1972–1973), pp. 21–24.

14. *Time and Tide* 36 (3rd December, 1955), p. 1561.

15. 'Tolkien's Creative Technique: *Beowulf* and *The Hobbit*', *Orcrist* 7 (1972–1973), pp. 16–20. This essay is based on Professor Christensen's doctoral dissertation, '*Beowulf* and *The Hobbit:* Elegy Into Fantasy in J.R.R. Tolkien's Creative Technique' (University of Southern California, 1969).

16. '*The Lord of the Rings*: The Novel as Traditional Romance'. See Note 3 above.

17. From a letter to Caroline Whitman Everett published in her M.A. thesis, 'The Imaginative Fiction of J.R.R. Tolkien' (Florida State University, 1957), p. 87.

18. They can be found in Tolkien's original manuscripts, which are in the Library Archives of Marquette University in Milwaukee.

19. Thomson, *op. cit.*, p. 49.

20. In much of this analysis, particularly in broad outline, I am indebted to C.S. Lewis's seminal review, 'The Dethronement of Power', *Time and Tide* 36 (22nd October, 1955), pp. 1373–74; reprinted in Neil D. Isaacs and Rose A. Zimbardo, eds., *Tolkien and the Critics* (South Bend: University of Notre Dame Press, 1968), pp. 12–16. There is also some debt to Randel Helms's brilliant essay, 'The Structure and Aesthetic of Tolkien's *Lord of the Rings*', delivered in 1970 at the first Mythcon of the Mythopoeic Society and published in *Mythcon I Proceedings* (1971), pp. 5–8.

21. J.R.R. Tolkien, *The Lord of the Rings* (New York: Ballantine, 1965). In three volumes. Volume I: *The Fellowship of the Ring*. Volume II: *The Two Towers*. Volume III: *The Return of the King*. Citations are given in the text by volume and page, for instance: II, p. 86. This procedure unfortunately reinforces the notion of this work as a 'trilogy', but this notion is too well established to be set aside here, for all that it ought to be.

22. Gandalf calls himself "a servant of the Secret Fire, wielder of the flame of Anor" (I, p. 429); he is the guardian of the Ring of Fire, one of the Three Rings of the Elves, given to him that "with it you may rekindle hearts in a world that grows chill" (III, p. 456); he scorches Weathertop with light and flame (I, p. 346), provides fire on Caradhras with the remark that the action plainly indicates to any observer who it is that is there (I, p. 380), drives away a wolf pack with fire (I, p. 390), and so forth. Even his toys are the fireworks he provides for Bilbo's party in the shire (I, p. 51).

23. *The Hobbit* (New York: Ballantine, 1966), pp. 270, 273.

24. For a discussion of Frodo as dreamer and visionary (and no one else in the romance has so many dreams or such varied ones), see Paul H. Kocher, *Master of Middle-earth: The Fiction of J.R.R. Tolkien* (Boston: Houghton Mifflin., 1972), pp. 119–121.

25. For a discussion of the nature of Tom Bombadil, see Gracia Fay Ellwood, *Good News from Tolkien's Middle Earth: Two Essays on the 'Applicability' of The Lord of the Rings* (Grand Rapids: Eerdmans, 1970), pp. 104–08.

26. An earlier version of this essay was published as 'The Interlace and Professor Tolkien: Medieval Narrative Technique in *The Lord of the Rings*', *Orcrist* 1 (1966–1967), pp. 26–49.

7

Narrative Pattern in *The Fellowship of the Ring*

DAVID M. MILLER

Like *The Hobbit, The Lord of the Rings* is a tale of 'there and back again', with various digressive adventures upon the way. Thus the setting of the three volumes is the road, a setting lending itself especially well to the narrative structure of the picaresque novel. Down this road a central character moves through adventure after adventure, perhaps learning and maturing as he goes, but encountering each experience essentially afresh. Picaresque episodes are essentially isolated, influencing those which follow primarily by thrusting the catalyst-hero farther along his path. Several adventures in *The Hobbit* fit this pattern. The road goes on and on, reaching to the Lonely Mountain, to the Crack of Doom, and to the Grey Havens. Even though Beorn appears at the battle of the five armies and the three trolls remain as wayside statues to frighten young travelers, the trolls and Beorn exist primarily for their own sakes. If both episodes were removed, they would be missed primarily because they are delightful in themselves. The structure, the sequence, and the significance of *The Hobbit* would be scarcely altered.

However, *The Lord of the Rings* should not be viewed as either a collection of tales or a more unified picaresque story. Although the goblins' capture of Bilbo in *The Hobbit* initially appears to be an entertaining digression, the Gollum episode cannot be removed without substantially altering Bilbo's development. These episodes indicate the basic distinction between an episodic picaresque and a unified structure. *The Lord of the Rings* has an extraordinarily unified structure which is evident from the economy of the narrative techniques used. We may quite properly ask, How does *this* move the Ring on its journey from Hobbiton to Mordor?, a question that implies disapproval of retrograde motions and of digressive adventures unless they have demonstrable utility for the larger movement of the tale, and receive a satisfactory explanation.

The most important narrative device in the *Lord of the Rings* is a quest. This in itself is not what it might seem to be because Tolkien's quest is not picaresque. Rather than seeking a dragon hoard (as did Bilbo) or the Grail (as did Arthur's knights), Frodo must throw away the most powerful magic yet remaining in Middle-earth. The peculiarities inherent in this reversal help Tolkien use familiar materials and situations in a fresh manner. The achievement of wealth is not the goal, and since the journey is not toward God, but toward evil, the traditional Christian assimilation of pagan heroic adventure is not relevant. This basic reversal is crucial. The nine walkers seek neither the gifts of this world, nor the illumination of holy beatitude: rather, they search for human independence. The destruction of the Ring of evil and the departure of elves and wizards narrow the scope of contending forces so as to bring the limited powers of humanity into a greater prominence. By humanity here I mean both men and hobbits. Rather than being simply the final straw which will tip the balance between massive forces, humanity becomes the central power itself. To this extent, *The Lord of the Rings* is a creation myth: it explains how the world got to be the way it is. The costly success of Frodo's quest does not provide "one greater Man" to restore the "blissful seat," but it does result in man's increased independence from the powers of both light and darkness.[1] In this regard, an incident in 'The Scouring of the Shire', the spreading of Galadriel's dust and the planting of the Mallorn tree, is often overlooked. The last thing Sam does is to take the few remaining motes in the box and blow them to the winds. This seems to me to signal the dissolution of a kind of order in which magic, white or black, is a major factor.

The basic reversal of the quest distinguishes *The Lord of the Rings* from most quests, whether medieval or modern. The quest moves away from magic, illumination, or extrasensory powers, toward the common man, the common-sense mode of the Western rational tradition. There is a similarity with the final episode in *Beowulf.* But the final guard of the treasure (the Smaug of *The Lord of the Rings)* is given a relatively minor role, whether you consider that final guard to be Shelob or the Silent Watchers of Cirith Ungol. Perhaps in another sense, we might say the final guard of the Ring is some sort of internal combination of Sméagol-Gollum-Frodo. The actual guards of the treasure are Frodo and the company. Indeed, what happens to the quest now is that the pieces are getting twisted. The Ring is kept in fear and hate, rather than with loving or even lusting reverence. The quest, in traditional terms, is Sauron's, not Frodo's, and the Black Riders have become the errant knights seeking the holy of holies. Further, the actual guards of the Ring do not wait passively to be attacked like a dragon curled around a tree with golden apples; like the proverbial dog in the manger, they can neither use the Ring nor allow it to be used. The full implications of these reversals embrace a larger subject than this brief essay can attempt. Here I can only make a tentative first step toward seeking in *The Fellowship of the Ring* elements which will lead toward a fuller understanding of the meaning of Tolkien's myth.

The Map and the Journey

Unlike most authors, Tolkien provides a special tool for examining narrative structure—one at the back of each volume. If a straight line is drawn on Tolkien's map from Hobbiton to Mount Doom, and if the actual path of the Ring is plotted on the same map, we have at once a graphic illustration of what might be called the narrative texture of *The Lord of the Rings.* The straight line represents the final direction of the tale, while the convoluted tracks of Frodo represent those individual circumstances that move it forward and give it substance. Each divergence from the straight line should be artistically desirable and result in an advance worth the delay. Understanding the reasons for Tolkien's digressions should increase our perception of unity in the story. We may discover that some episodes are picaresque, existing primarily for their own sakes, but we need not assume that this will be true.

The most obvious obstacles to taking the direct route are topographical: mountains, river, marshes, and forests often make it impossible. Such features are particularly important in Middle-earth, where a tree may not be simply a tree. It is not just the peoples of Middle-earth who are endangered by Sauron—Gollum fears that "he" may well eat the whole world itself. The very rocks and valleys, in their fashion, fight for existence; like the creatures of Middle-earth, some have been twisted to Sauron's will.

The initial destination of the Ring is not Mordor but Rivendell, and in terms of the overall pattern of the journey, this first stage appears to be a major digression. But it we use Tolkien's division of *The Fellowship of the Ring* into two books as a guide, an interesting result appears. If you draw a line from Hobbiton to Mount Doom, you do so because that is where the journey goes. But in fact the travelers originally head for Rivendell. Then they move south. This Hobbiton-to-Rivendell-to-the-South journey forms a kind of triangle with the base as the direct line and the angles marked by the ends of Tolkien's books. This division indicates the formal relationship between the map and the story. A straight line from Hobbiton to Rivendell, the terminus of Book I, and another line from Rivendell to Rauros, the end of the Book II, forms, with the straight line from Hobbiton to Mordor, a remarkably symmetrical triangle. The East Road veers from a straight course to Rivendell only twice, at the Old Forest and at Weathertop. The journey of Book I is strikingly economical in direction if not in time. We shall return shortly to its few digressions.

The second side of the triangle, stretching from Rivendell to Rauros, passes through Lothlórien and, from that point on, parallels the flow of Anduin in much the same way that the line of Book I parallels the East Road. The major digression of Book II is that which takes the company through Moria. Like the digressions of Book I, the journey in the dark plunges the company into the abyss of history. And when the Balrog is waked, we discover that we are archeologists as well as investigators of what happened to dwarf civilization. This digression anticipates, in miniature, the climax of the trilogy. Gandalf, like the Ring, must be hurled into the flame; Frodo must give up his powerful aid in order to gain freedom for himself and the peoples of Middle-earth. As in the larger pattern, Gandalf and the Balrog cancel each other so that lesser powers may hold sway.

As soon as the walkers escape from Moria, they move as directly as possible back to the direct route line to Mordor. Since the goal of the Ring has been settled by the conference at Rivendell, there can no longer be a question of its general direction. Frodo forces it toward Orodruin with all the clumsy persistence of a large man trying to thread a needle. But Elrond has not made it clear whether or not the Ring may journey to Minas Tirith before it enters Mordor. It is significant that an extension of the line from Rivendell to Rauros would miss Mordor and pass through Minas Tirith. Thus the map points up the mixed motives of the company and counterpoints what we learn from the story itself: had the will of Boromir prevailed, the Ring would not have reached Orodruin. We learn that Boromir would have undoubtedly been corrupted by the Ring if he had attempted to use its power to defeat Sauron in battle.

Until the Ring reaches Rauros, no decision need be made. The journey south on the river fits the goals of Aragorn, of Boromir, and of Frodo. But at Rauros a crisis occurs—a crisis indicated on the map. Every step in Boromir's direction leads away from the volcano. Boromir falls under the evil influence of the Ring. Responsibility for the quest again falls to a lesser figure—Frodo. The dissolution of the Fellowship effectively concludes Book I.

Volume II is organized differently. The neat triangle of *The Fellowship of the Ring* gives way in the next two volumes to a number of eccentric spirals, one set on each side of the river. Like the divided company, the circles seem to form independently. They are reunited, eventually, at the climactic battle before the gates of Mordor.

In passing it may be noted that there is no path back from Orodruin. The road ends there. Gwaihir's intercession is necessary. He picks up the spent hobbits and flies them out. The conclusion of the narrative, the 'happy' ending, seems thus to superimposed upon a tragedy—a tragedy which is revealed simply by looking at the paths people follow in their quest. The story seems to demand that Frodo plunge, with the Ring, into the Crack of Doom. And in fact, not all of Frodo returns from Mordor: that can be seen in 'The Scouring of the Shire'. Frodo is no longer a whole hobbit—he has given up his hobbitness. Pippin and Merry have drunk of the entwash: they too are no longer mere hobbits. Sam is the least affected of all the hobbits, yet he also is not the same. In this I think we find Tolkien's suggestion of a basic strength in yeomanry: the idea that the fellow who can draw the clothyard with his bow can defeat any ten frog-eating Frenchmen, and so on. Somehow, there is a reservoir here to be drawn upon in future generations of man.

But that is rather beside the point: the point is that the logic of the map demands a tragedy. If Gollum is Frodo's *alter ego*—which I think he is—the tale is a tragedy of the classical kind; though the purging of one's 'Gollumness' makes of that tragedy a sort of divine comedy. Tolkien's map points up the underlying tragedy: the path ends in a volcano.

These lines of speculation are raised only in passing, though a great deal might be learned by examining the contrapuntal structure of the spirals of movement east and west of the river. Let us instead return to a detailed examination of the spatial, thematic, and temporal structures of Volume I.

The East Road fits Frodo's purpose very well; he has only to join it south of Bywater, turn left, and he will eventually come to the Ford of Bruinen. His reasons for not doing so make up the narrative texture of Book I. The first digression from the road leads the Ring south through Woodyend across Stock Brook to Buckland. Its utility is largely expository. We begin with the ordinariness of a hobbit in the familiar and thoroughly unmagical Shire: before the Ring arrives in Buckland, we have been gently introduced to both Black Riders and elves. We also learn that forces for good and evil, distant and vastly more powerful than a hobbit, are concerned with Frodo's stewardship of the Ring. Gandalf has described the magnitude of the struggle to Frodo, whose fears are as those of a child listening to a ghost story; the light of day clears his fear. And we, the reader, are guided by Frodo's response.[2] We perceive the truth of Gandalf's statements as we perceive the truth through Frodo's eyes. We are tutored so that what might have been fantasy in the bad sense is made artistically believable.

Nine Cycles of Danger and Rescue

The first stage of the journey, from Hobbiton to Crick Hollow, sets a pattern of events which is repeated at least nine times in Book I. A conference held in tranquility (with plenty of food and drink) prompts a movement of the Ring. The hobbits then blunder more or less light-heartedly into danger. Unexpected aid arrives, aid that is exactly appropriate to the danger. Disaster is narrowly averted, and the feasting tranquillity is momentarily restored. For the sake of convenience, I have presented this cycle in a chart:

Conference in Tranquillity	Blundering Journey	Danger	Unexpected Aid
Gandalf and Frodo	Woodyend	Black Rider	Elves
Elves and Frodo	Stock Brook	Black Rider	Farmer Maggot
Maggot and Frodo	Ferry (no blunder)	Black Rider (vague)	Hobbit Fellowship
Frodo and Hobbits	Old Forest	Old Man Willow	Bombadil
Bombadil and Frodo	Barrow Downs	Barrow Wight	Bombadil (expected)
Bombadil and Frodo	Prancing Pony	Black Rider	Strider Party
Strider and Frodo	Weathertop	Black Riders	Frodo himself Strider (healer)
Strider and Frodo	Last Bridge	Black Riders	Glorfindel
Glorfindel and Strider	Ford of Bruinen	Black Riders	Gandalf, Elrond, Bruinen

Several observations may be made about these cycles. First, each conference is associated with food; the movement is from feast to famine to feast. The symbolic pattern of eating seen most clearly in the struggle between Sméagol and Gollum in Volume II is established. In Middle-earth, you are what you eat, or perhaps you eat what you are. Second, each danger is total; a single failure would be final. Yet the hobbits' sense of danger is minimal. Only gradually do they realize the significance of the quest. Sam, perhaps, does not understand the scope of the quest until he and Frodo cross the plateau of Gorgoroth. Third, the unexpected aid requires a catalytic courage from those in danger. Thus the free will of the hobbits is maintained in a battle with forces far greater than their own powers. Tolkien works out conflicting themes of fate and free will. Gandalf, Galadriel, and the One help those who help themselves. Fourth, the unexpected aid is a response, in kind, to the particular danger. In Book I, the aid is the existent force for good appropriate to the land in which the danger occurs. The hobbits ignite the latent resistance to Sauron's tyranny in the lands through which they pass. The final danger of Book I is the massing of Black Riders at the ford. The responsive aid comes from several levels of existence: from Strider (man), from Glorfindel (elf), from Gandalf (wizard), from Elrond (halfelven), and from Loudwater (nature). Yet without a supreme effort by Frodo the aid is useless. In the dash to the Ford of Bruinen he is stripped of all aid (except the horse). Five, the rescuer in one cycle becomes the counselor in the next. The small cycles of Book I form a single large cycle as Gandalf, the first counselor, returns as first counselor in Book II. Frodo's importance grows as his resistance is seen to be adequate to the ever-increasing danger. He receives aid from increasingly powerful levels of being as he himself is able to act as a more powerful catalyst.

The divergences from this cyclic pattern are themselves instructive. After the feast and council at Crickhollow, the hobbits plan their own rescue; this is unusual. They enlist hobbit ingenuity by disguising Fatty Bolger as Frodo. The stratagem is pathetic, for he runs screaming denial the moment danger appears. The Shire is utterly unable to stand against the power of Sauron; even one Black Rider is far too much for it. Yet by the time Frodo reaches Weathertop, the battle can, however foolishly, be joined by a single hobbit lost in the spiritual darkness of Sauron's power. And when the hobbits return to the Shire, they are capable of handling Sharkey and his ruffians, if only because the greater powers have been destroyed or withdrawn.

While the climax of Frodo's physical courage occurs at Weathertop, the climactic aid does not arrive until the Ford of Bruinen is reached. Between Weathertop and Bruinen, Frodo must simply endure. The Ring-bearer is to be a suffering servant, not a conquering hero. The events of Book I suggest that physical courage is but the first, and minimum, requirement of the quest. The cost of that endurance is demonstrated at the close of Volume III. Frodo is virtually useless in the practical affair of scouring the shire. Finally, he must leave Middle-earth.

In the 'Danger' column of the cyclic chart, the episode with Tom Bombadil stands out as an anomaly. The cycle is there, but the adventures with Old Man Willow and the Barrow Wight do not move the Ring down the road to Rivendell, nor do the dangers directly threaten the Ring. The hobbits travel at least four times as far as if they had remained on the East Road, and they are not forced off that road by natural topography. The Old Forest passage is seemingly the least economical section of Book I. Aside from the hobbits' obvious desire to evade the Black Riders, there seems little reason for the two episodes. Neither Old Man Willow nor the Barrow-wight wants Frodo's Ring, and the rescuer, Bombadil, is wholly beyond the Ring's power. Further, the episodes of wight and willow are geographically separate from the rest of Book I.

Through Layers of Time

The adventures with Tom Bombadil appear to be a genuine digression, an episode in which narrative flow is subordinate to other goals. Tolkien gives several hints as to their utility. The first, typically, comes in the names: *Old* Forest, *Old* Man Willow, Tom as *Eldest*. When the hobbits enter the forest, it is as though they had broken through a crust in time. Like archeologists chipping through layers of centuries, they dip into the first age of Middle-earth. There they discover a remnant of that First Age when trees ruled. Tom and Goldberry may be Mother and Father Nature, or they may be only the eldest of humans; clearly, they are anachronisms, left over from the First Age. As living artifacts they are completely outside the narrative flow. Their structural importance is temporal, not geographical.

The Lord of the Rings has, of course, the usual sort of time— that which is indicated by a sequence of events, by mutability.

It is closely associated with the journey motif and has a kind of psychological topography, complete with mountains, caves, and rivers. Like the journey itself, time spurts and lags with discernible rhythm. Rivendell and Lothlórien are timeouts in both movement and calendar.

Bombadil, however, represents a different sense of time. The Old Forest is not merely left over from the First Age; it is the First Age. Like the eyes of Fangorn, the forest is a well of time. The reader learns that the evils Frodo must meet are but manifestations of an evil principle against which creation has always struggled. The effort of Frodo is not unique, yet it is all important. He struggles not only for the present, which must pass in any case, and the future, but also for the past. To see Tom and Goldberry fall under the shadow of Mordor is to see the strength and purity of earth's origins enslaved. Their defeat would deny the worth of a past in which beauty and freedom existed. In a curious way, Frodo must battle to save not only the length and breadth of the world, but the depth of history as well. Sauron as an individual is merely a shadow upon the light of the moment, but Sauron as a principle has the power to eliminate even the past existence of light: Like the preservation of virginity in a heroic romance, a victory ensures only the following day's battle, but a single loss is total. Ultimately it is Frodo who saves Tom—not in the sense of continuing Tom's existence into the future, but of allowing him to cease to exist without perversion.

The Barrow-wight episode is a similar, but more complex, exercise in temporal archeology. As the willow represents the First Age, the wight represents the Second. Frodo's struggle in the barrow is, in fact, a miniature version of the Ring quest acted out in the Second Age of Middle-earth. When Frodo passes the standing stone, he moves through a doorway in time and becomes a part of the defeat which created the wights from free men. "The men of Carn Dûm came on us at night, and we were worsted. Ah! the spear in my heart!" he cries. Carn Dûm was the stronghold, in the Second Age, of the Witch King of Angmar; the success of his minions resulted in the spiritual enslavement of the peoples of the Barrow-downs. It is also a dim forecast of what would happen should Sauron triumph. When Frodo strikes off the ghostly hand, he anticipates the thrust which Merry gives the Lord of Minas Morgul and recalls the cutting off of Sauron's finger by Isildur. His call for Bombadil's aid (a call from the

Second Age to the First) is like his own later call to Elbereth (from the Third Age to the Second). In scattering the treasure, destroying the barrow, and banishing the wight, Bombadil anticipates the destruction of Barad-dûr and the windy dissolution of Sauron (mimicked later in the defeat and death of Saruman in the Shire).

Help comes to Frodo only after he has demonstrated his own will to resist evil, and those who rescue him are themselves galvanized by that will. Presumably Bombadil could have destroyed the barrow and freed the wight on any one of ten thousand previous days. It is Frodo who brings the saving power of the First Age to free the Second Age of an evil so that the wight, in the Third Age, may cease to exist.

In the Bombadil episode, Tolkien has sent Frodo to the kind of school Merlin provided for Arthur. To understand wights, wraiths, and living trees, one must almost become a wraith himself. And yet the schooling is perilous. When Gandalf learns of the barrow episode, he is horrified, recognizing that had Frodo failed in the barrow, it would have been as though Sauron had never lost the Ring, as though the Third Age of Middle-earth were not ended, but canceled. All this makes very little impression upon the hobbits. They wonder at Tom, they shudder at the wight, and they go cheerfully off to a party at Bree, quite unsobered and seemingly uninstructed.

The events of Book I form not so much a cycle as a spiral. The stakes are constantly increased and the gamblers become increasingly self-aware. The weaving through both time and space of Tolkien's myth makes *The Lord of the Rings* a tale for all seasons. A map, a ruler, and a pencil provide one key to understanding the lure of Middle Earth.

NOTES TO CHAPTER 7

1. For an extended discussion, see David M. Miller, 'The Moral Universe of J.R.R. Tolkien', in *Tolkien Papers, Mankato Studies in English* 2:1(1967), pp. 51–62.

2. See my 'Hobbits: Common Lens for Heroic Experience', *Tolkien Journal, XI-Orcrist* 3 (1969), pp. 11–15.

8

'The Scouring of the Shire': Tolkien's View of Fascism

ROBERT PLANK

My primary interest is not in the literary value of Tolkien's work, that is, declaring it good or bad. Rather, I am interested in approaching it as a product of the human imagination, in the same way that, as a psychiatric social worker, I would study a client's story about himself or one of his dreams. Using this approach, I hope to shed new light on the trilogy itself. The degree to which this method can succeed is, admittedly, questionable, but I hope that any discussion of the methods, if not the results, will be fruitful.

A Realistic Story

With these pitfalls in mind, I will concentrate on 'The Scouring of the Shire', Chapter 8 of Book VI of *The Lord of the Rings*, the last-but-one chapter of the entire trilogy, because I feel that it presents the most flexible ground for my approach. In reading *The Lord of the Rings,* you have probably noticed that 'The Scouring of the Shire' is a separate and independent episode, a unit that pretty much stands by itself. Yet it is almost impossible to read it with enjoyment and understanding, either alone or with the rest of the trilogy. This chapter is, I feel, also fundamentally different from the rest of the book. It serves as an epilogue to the tremendous adventures, which are over: the great war has been won, the world has been saved, the heroes are coming home.

Right here we run into a question of method. Many attempts have been made to explain Tolkien as a creator of myths. Although the mythical or archetypical approach may illuminate Tolkien's work in general, it fails to give a meaningful explanation of 'The Scouring of the Shire'.

The motif of the hero coming home from victory in battle is of course a very old one. Tolkien could have patterned his story of the return of the classical hero after Agamemnon, who is killed by his unfaithful wife Clytemnestra—or any number of such heroes. As his heroes come home, they do not find that their lovers have been unfaithful or that anything has happened during their absence to bring them personal tragedy. Sam will marry his Rosie. Frodo will go to his fate which has by this time assumed its final form beyond any human power to change it.

But this is not to say that they find the Shire as they left it— far from it. Yet the changes have been political rather than personal. The return of Frodo and his band to the Shire is in this respect similar to the homecoming of Ulysses in Homer's *Odyssey* (with different personal and sexual connotations).

It is equally important that 'The Scouring of the Shire' differs from other episodes in Tolkien's work in respect to the question of fantasy versus realism. *The New York Times Book Review* recently carried an article on paperbacks favored by young readers. Five novels were listed as outstanding: Vonnegut's *Cat's Cradle,* Heinlein's *Stranger in a Strange Land,* Hesse's *Steppenwolf,* Herbert's *Dune,* and *The Lord of the Rings.* The narrator comments:

> These are all heady books, not exactly escapist but something close to it—verbal and fantastic trips through other worlds, other realities. Their heroes all possess marvelous or occult talents. . . .

The reviewer describes the dreamlike quality of the works, their heroes' unusual powers and the mixture of the real and the fantastic in these stories. Although this describes Tolkien's work in general it does not, quite obviously, function as a description of 'The Scouring of the Shire'.

The outstanding characteristic of 'The Scouring of the Shire' is that miracles do not happen, the laws of nature are in full and undisputed force, the actors in the drama are all human (technically, most of them are hobbits while some are men, but the difference is played down so radically it is immaterial). You will notice that even though Saruman has been a powerful magician, he does not use magic at any point in that episode: whatever headway he makes, he makes as a politician rather than as a sorcerer. In other words, 'The Scouring of the Shire' is not fantasy. It is essentially a realistic story. The only point where the laws of nature are suspended is the dissolution of Saruman's body when he is killed; but this happens at the very end, after the plot has run its course and the restoration of liberty in the Shire has been completed.

Now of course, when I call 'The Scouring of the Shire' a realistic story, I do not mean to imply that events are described exactly as they would happen in reality. Tolkien gives us the essence of reality by altering many of its circumstances, especially by miniaturizing it. His story is a realistic parable of reality. But what is the reality he depicts?

The Shire is almost unrecognizable to the returning veterans. The changes amount to a political and economical revolution, as far as these rather high-sounding words can be applied to the small scale of the Shire. The economic changes are an outgrowth of the political changes—they can only be effected by the use, or rather misuse, of political power. But we are given to understand that the economic changes are the real aim of those who have seized political power and changed its nature.

The political changes were not essentially constitutional changes. The laws have been perverted more than amended. The traditional offices have not been abolished, but new power is wielded by a new ruling group. The essential political innovation is the rise of an unprecedented police force, headed by the Chief Shirriff. The character of government is totally altered while its forms are not markedly changed. Whereas before the Shire enjoyed an easy-going *laissez faire* regime, with maximum freedom and a minimum of government interference, the new regime operates through monstrously expanded restrictive rules, enforced by equally monstrously expanded military and paramilitary forces. These troops are not productive; in fact, they do not contribute anything that would be in any way necessary if the regime were different. All their work serves their own selfish ends: the purpose of government is plainly to maintain, consolidate, and expand its own power.

Even if they were not motivated by ill-will toward the citizenry—which they are—these troops would have to consume a large part of the goods and services that were formerly available to the people. But they do make themselves inimical first by taxation, then confiscation, then barefaced robbery. A problem arises that apparently was unknown in the Shire before: What should be done to a citizen who 'talks back' to the government? The solution is simple: He is imprisoned and often beaten.

Fascism in the Shire

The economy is now controlled. Under the pretext of 'fair sharing', a system of government requisitions and of rationing has evolved. Shortages result, and when consumer goods are in short supply they have a way of ending up, to nobody's great surprise, with the privileged militia. Farmer Cotton has summed it up better than I could:

> There wasn't no smoke [tobacco] left, save for the Men; and the Chief didn't hold with beer, save for his Men, and closed all the inns; and everything except rules got shorter and shorter. . . .

It may seem improbable that such a regime could ever establish itself, either in the Shire or in a more sizable country. But history has a trick of making the improbable happen. The sorry state of the Shire looks like a portrait—or maybe caricature—of something that actually happened in fairly recent history. It is a perfectly recognizable portrait of fascism.

Democracy has been simply defined as 'government of the people, by the people, and for the people'. Fascism is its antithesis. It is government of a clique, by the clique, against the people—like the government of the Shire before the scouring. Note the details that logically follow from the basic principle: the proliferation of the military and bureaucratic arms of government, the control of the economy, the pretense of legality, the cynical disregard for freedom and the rights of individual citizens, the violence, the brutality.

Depending on your political orientation, you may be inclined to see in Tolkien's description of the corruption of the Shire a portrait of communism rather than fascism. I think this would be a mistake. While it is of course true that communism and fascism have many features in common, and while some of the particulars that I have listed may apply even more rigorously to communism than to fascism, there are also marked differences between the two systems; and Tolkien clearly indicates some distinguishing characteristics. Communism at least starts out with a lofty ideal (whatever may become of it later), but the group that usurps power in the Shire does not even pretend to idealism. All we hear is an occasional platitude, "This country wants waking up and setting to rights." Communism is based on a theory of class struggle, while fascism preaches the unity of the people, which means in practice that everybody is treated equally badly, and this is certainly true in the Shire. And just as fascism got its start with the help of certain upper-class elements who thought it would serve them as a bulwark against what they were pleased to call the greed of the working man, so the ruffians get their first foothold from the Sackville-Bagginses. Let me again quote Farmer Cotton:

> He'd funny ideas, had Pimple. Seems he wanted to own everything himself, and then order other folk about . . . Folk got angry, but he had his answer. A lot of Men, ruffians mostly, came with great waggons, some to carry off the goods south-away, and others to stay. And more came. And before we knew where we were they were planted here and there all over the Shire. . . .

And just as those who helped the Fascists and the Nazis into power saw their mistake when it was too late, so Pimple—pardon me, Mr. Lotho Sackville-Baggins—goes to his reward. He is murdered and perhaps eaten.

This brings us to the enigmatic figure of Saruman. There has been much discussion whether or not his overlord, Sauron, represents Hitler—an impression some readers cannot avoid. However, another interpretation has considerable merit: Saruman bears two striking resemblances to Mussolini. Mussolini started his career as a local labor leader and became the most ruthless oppressor of the labor movement. Saruman also is a turncoat. Secondly, just like Mussolini, Saruman comes to a miserable end, utterly lacking in the theatrical glory of a *Götterdämmerung*.

This is not to say that Saruman *is* Mussolini. I am suggesting something more basic and at the same time much less definite

The problem of fascism was as much a pervasive part of the mental climate of Europe then as (for instance) the problem of atomic energy was a part of our mental climate after World War II, or the problem of race relations more recently. It was not hard for a writer to borrow traits from the chief of Fascism in the design of a character; it would have been more difficult to keep that sinister shadow out of his inspiration.

The objection has been raised that *The Lord of the Rings* was conceived in its totality, and to a great extent written, prior to World War II. But the strength of this disagreement is more apparent than real, for the war was the high-water mark rather than the birth of these movements. We must not confuse the time of their rise with the time when broad public opinion in the United States woke up to seeing them for what they were.

It was a summer day in 1924 that the socialist deputy Giacomo Matteotti, who had become the principle spokesman for the opposition in the Italian parliament, was murdered. Tracks led directly to the head of the government, Mussolini. Clearly, the deed had been committed on his orders, or at least in order to please him. Europe was shocked. Fascism, which until then had been looked at as some sort of Italian opera, stood revealed as a brutal threat to freedom and civilization.

To perceive this, and to act on the perception, were, alas, two different things. Fascism was not overthrown from within. A coalition of the other powers toppled it, but they did so only when they had no other choice left. It seems clear enough in retrospect that had the effort been made earlier, it would have required much less sacrifice. One of the greatest catastrophes in history could have been almost avoided. Why wasn't it?

Sharkey Toppled

Tolkien presents reasons why there was no effective resistance to fascism in the Shire; they make instructive and melancholy reading. One reason is cowardice: as one of the guardsmen utters some rather mild gripes, he is shut up by his comrades: "You know talk o'that sort isn't allowed. The Chief will hear of it, and we'll all be in trouble." Another reason is lack of solidarity: "I've been itching for trouble all this year," says my favorite witness, Farmer Cotton, "but folks wouldn't help." And, "if we all got angry together something might be done," says another hobbit, but to say so he lowers his voice. The third reason is the most interesting and the most melancholy: "I am sorry Mr. Merry, but we have orders." We heard something like this in the courtroom in Nuremberg.

In spite of his clear insight into the forces that hamstring resistance, and in spite of the fact that he wrote 'The Scouring of the Shire' after World War II, that is, history had drawn those rivers of blood, sweat, and tears that an even more famous British writer had foretold, Tolkien still describes the overthrow of a tyrannical government as a quick and easy job. This seems surprising, but it can be explained in part by Tolkien's choice of such a very small political unit as the Shire and in part by the mildness of his description. I have said before that his picture of the Lotho-Saruman regime is a caricature of fascism; I must add that any earthly fascist regime has been much worse than what Tolkien shows.

Another reason perhaps why Tolkien thinks it easy to overthrow an oppressive government is that he overrates the impact of courage. Frodo and his friends have courage but little else, and entrenched power falls before them like a house of cards. These heroes do not persuade, they do not convince anybody. They rally the people, but the people have already been on their side. Yet discussion and persuasion are the lifeblood of democracy. And courage is more an aristocratic than a democratic virtue.

I would not think it rash to conclude that Tolkien opposes fascism as a conservative rather than as a democrat. Here is what he himself says, in his foreword to a reissue of *The Lord of the Rings:*

> It has been supposed by some that 'The Scouring of the Shire' reflects the situation in England at the time when I was finishing my tale. [That would be, as he told us in another passage, about 1949.] It does not. It is an essential part of the plot, foreseen from the outset, though in the event modified by the character of Saruman as developed in the story without, need I say, any allegorical significance or contemporary political reference whatsoever. It has indeed some basis in experience, though slender (for the economic situation was entirely different), and much further back. The country in which I lived in childhood was being shabbily destroyed before I was ten, in days when motor-cars were rare objects (I had never seen one) and men were still building subur-

ban railways. Recently I saw in a paper a picture of the last decrepi-
tude of the once thriving corn-mill beside its pool that long ago
seemed to me so important. I never liked the looks of the Young
miller, but his father, the Old miller, had a black beard, and he was
not named Sandyman.

To me personally, this is a wonderful passage. I find it most
fascinating when a creative adult can trace his inspirations back
to childhood, especially when it is done with so much charm
and obvious sincerity—down to the seemingly irrelevant detail
of the miller's beard.

Tolkien's recollection accounts very fully for one peculiar-
ity of his story, one that I have so far refrained from mentioning, namely the emphasis, quite unusual for its time, on what
we would now call the deterioration of the environment. At
virtually every step his returning warriors come upon the evidence of the environmental crimes that have been committed
in their absence: old houses torn down and replaced by mean
new architecture; air and water polluted, gardens neglected;
and above all, trees wantonly destroyed. Tolkien gives the
impression that his heroes—and by extension, he himself—
must consider this a greater crime than what the government
did to people. But we know that the brutal disregard for the
environment is not specifically a sin of oppressive govern-
ments. It could be argued that unfettered liberalism has done
worse.

I am satisfied that I have brought out two points, one of
interest to Tolkien scholars, one more of interest to me. Readers
of Tolkien seem either to admire him or the think that he is a
fascist. To define more precisely where he stands may be of
some value for Tolkien scholarship. On the other hand, there is
the matter of differential diagnosis: to recognize fascism when
you see it and also to be able to recognize antifascism even if it
is of a variety you may not like, is a mark of a critical ability we
all need.

The connection between two basic themes in 'The Scouring
of the Shire' needs further clarification. Tolkien's childhood
memory explains why he would have the Shire environmentally
devastated while his heroes are away. It does not explain why
he would weave into his epic the story of the rise and fall of an
oppressive government. And why would he so emphatically

protest that his story contains "no contemporary political reference whatsoever"?

An answer could at best be speculative. Instead of attempting this, I shall leave it unanswered in the hopes that the results of my approach have been as provocative as my method.

9

Hell and The City:
Tolkien and the Traditions
of Western Literature

CHARLES A. HUTTAR

"We thinke that Paradise and Calvarie,/Christs Crosse, and Adams tree, stood in one place." Donne's words have puzzled source hunters, for they do not directly follow known legends.[1] Nevertheless, they show a sound instinct for translating myth into concrete images. In the 'Hymne to God my God, in my sicknesse' the poet participates in the mysterious yet common human experience—death. But in his Christian mind the descent into death is inseparable from a rising again. 'West' and 'East', sunset and sunrise, represent these twin movements. The reference of the poem expands as his personal descent and rising are given a backdrop showing the same pattern on a much larger scale: the fall of the entire human race in the first Adam and its redemption in the second.

> Looke Lord, and finde both Adams met in me;
> As the first Adams sweat surrounds my face,
> May the last Adams blood my soule embrace.

The theology is made concrete through the mythical geography. Donne has made the Cross and the Tree stand together at the one sacred spot, familiar to many widely scattered cultures, where earth and heaven meet.

In the myths the tree or pole at the 'earth navel', the axis of the world, can be climbed to heaven and it often reaches down to the depths of the underworld.[2] From this three-tiered arrangement comes the middleness of what the Anglo-Saxons called Middle-earth. The precise physical features of the cosmic navel vary in the versions of different primitive societies. Instead of a tree, the upward-pointing pillar may be a whole forest, or a garden; these may stand atop a mountain, or the mountain itself may represent the way to the gods; or it may be (or resemble) a man-made object—a ziggurat or other form of tower, a ladder (as in Jacob's dream), or a temple located at the center of a holy city. Often a hole provides a passage from earth to heaven, as in the roof of the Pueblo Indians' kiva, or permits access to the underworld through a tunnel, a labyrinth, or a cave. The mountain itself may be hollow, and in some legends, Paradise is found in these interior regions. However, the underworld is usually sinister, a place of darkness and death if not actually torment; although its entrance is in the heart of the beautiful garden, its surroundings are danger-ridden. For instance, it was here that the unwitting Proserpina "gathering flow'rs,/Herself a fairer flow'r, by gloomy Dis/Was gathered."[3] Yet out of the depths of Earth may also spring the Water of Life—in some versions from four streams, in others from the sacred river—flowing from the sap of the Tree or coming into the Garden from another source and disappearing into the ground to follow a winding subterranean course down to the sea.[4] The sea itself may be a prominent part of the whole scene, as with Mount Purgatory and the end of Ulysses's westward journey. His earlier adventures, in Homer, include Calypso's island, called "the navel of the sea," where the goddess lives in a great cave in which a fire perpetually burns.

Many of these images reappear in customs for the disposal of the dead—funeral pyres, cave burial, barrows, pyramids, mausoleums, and churchyards. The legendary old man in Chaucer's *Pardoner's Tale*, knocking with his staff at the door of "Mother Earth" that she might readmit him to the peace and security of existence in the bowels of the earth, illustrates the close alliance in imagery between the two mysteries of birth and death, how womb and tomb (linguists assure us the rime is no coincidence) complete a full cycle.

The Lord of the Rings is deeply indebted to this universe of images and derives much of its strength as mythography from a similar clustering of such images. I will proceed to investigate some of Tolkien's uses of this cluster of symbols in two particulars, the descent into hell and the image of the city.

I. The Descent into Hell

The journey to hell is one kind of universal quest myth—of what Joseph Campbell, following Joyce, calls the *monomyth*. "A hero ventures forth from the world of common day into a region of supernatural wonder: fabulous forces are there encountered and a fabulous victory is won: the hero comes back from this mysterious adventure with the power to bestow boons on his fellow man" (Campbell, p. 30). The hero's adventure has three stages, departure, initiation, and return; the first two comprise his journey to hell. He is singled out to be a hero, called to undertake the quest, given a choice to accept or refuse which is at the same time a test of whether or not he really qualifies. He then undergoes a series of further trials, wins through by supernatural aid, enters into the final deathlike struggle, and eventually emerges victorious. For all of this the hero receives no assurances, only the challenge to accept the call and at most a suggestion of the good that may result.[5]

Hell is underground, cut off from sunlight and warmth. Dark and hence unknown, it is a region of dread. Though sometimes synonymous with the grave, in the quest myth hell is not simply the dwelling place of the dead; far more terrifying is the knowledge that it is the abode of the monster himself—Death, or the monarch who holds powerful sway over all this mysterious realm, or evil in some embodiment.

Life itself may of course be seen as such a journey—"to be born is to begin to die."[6] It is from the warm, comfortable, womblike recesses of Bag End that Mr. Frodo Baggins, alias Mr. Underhill, is called to venture forth on "a very long road, into darkness" (I, p. 96). His setting out, having sold Bag End and concluded the affairs of his former life, resembles both a death and a birth. Clearer images of death follow quickly—he hides under covers in Farmer Maggot's wagon as in a hearse, leaves the Shire by a tunnel and enters the Old Forest, where monstrous trees block the way and the path inevitably leads down to "the centre from which all the queerness comes" (p. 124). There the hobbits are overcome by drowsiness which "seemed to be creeping out of the ground and up their legs" (p. 127) and

nearly entombed in the willow tree. After the companions leave
the house of Tom Bombadil, they skirt a land ridged with barrows, great burial mounds containing the treasures of ancient
men whose spirits still haunt them, as we learn from Merry's
delirium (p. 154). Once again some sinister force seems to prey
on the weakness of their own wills to deflect them into this new
danger. Like the Green Chapel of Sir Gawain's quest, which they
resemble, the barrows are a necessary stage in Frodo's initiation.
And they hear the marks by which hell is recognized: "standing
stones, pointing upward like jagged teeth out of green gums" (p.
148), a low door leading into the dark interior, and within, a
monster of greed and darkness whose touch is like ice. He turns
the other three hobbits "deathly pale," but Frodo must remain
conscious to confront both hopeless dread and the temptation
to escape with the Ring and leave the others to perish. He
passes the test. Attacking the Barrow-wight with the weapon
nearest to hand (like Beowulf in the monster's lair beneath the
lake), he sets in motion the series of events that bring deliver-
ance. The demon of the mound is exorcised by Tom Bombadil,
the treasure brought out of hiding and the spell broken.
Through Tom's instruction and their previous experiences
underground, the hobbits are wiser and better prepared for
future encounters.

Rivendell is the interlude between the first and second stages
of Frodo's quest. Here he learns enough about the nature of his
call so that his decision at the Council to accept the burden of
the quest is a real choice. Rivendell is a notable place. It is no
world navel, for it lacks the vertical connections with the heights
and depths, but horizontally it is a center of Middle-earth.
"There's something of everything here," Sam is to say much later
(III, pp. 264f.), "the Shire and the Golden Wood and Gondor and
kings' houses and inns and meadows and mountains all mixed."

THE RISK-FILLED ENTRANCE

As the sun reaches the lowest point and begins to climb each day
higher above the horizon, the fellowship begin their its journey
to take the ring to Mordor. Three months of winter adventure lie
ahead. Their first task is to get beyond the Misty Mountains.
There are two possible routes, over or through. The fellowship
attempt the pass of Caradhras, but a blizzard with seemingly
active malevolence turns them back. Once more the Ring-bearer

is guided inescapably toward an underground journey by a "dark and secret way" (I, p. 301) which even Aragorn dreads—the road under the mountains, Khazad-dûm, the Dwarrowdelf, the Mines of Moria, "now called the Black Pit" (p. 296).

Before the door to Moria lies a dark lake, fully as forbidding as the lake into which Beowulf descended. Gandalf's remark (p. 315) could be Anglo-Saxon in its understatement. "None of the Company, I guess, will wish to swim this gloomy water at the end of the day. It has an unwholesome look." In this Avernus of Tolkien's there dwells a guardian monster quite as threatening and dangerous as any Briareus encountered by Aeneas. It "has crept . . . out of dark waters under the mountains." It is a thing of evil, "older and fouler . . . than Orcs" (p. 323). Frodo very narrowly escapes its tentacles.[7]

At the entrance to this hell there is an enchanted door that is invisible until spells are spoken and opens only at the correct password. It is characteristic of Tolkien's non-epic that the secret word, once perceived, should be so disarmingly simple: "Say 'Friend' and enter" (p. 322). Except for minor changes the situation is parallel to the *Aeneid* and its golden bough, or to any other myth in which a living person who would dare the underground passage must offer some evidence that he is indeed the hero who has been called.

No sooner has the company passed through than the gate clashes shut, swung by the angry tentacles of the guardian and blocked forever. I see two kinds of significance in this. Earlier, Aragorn has said, "The road may lead to Moria, but how can we hope it will lead through Moria?" (p. 309). This question now becomes vital. Aeneas had been warned that to reascend was difficult; for the Ring companions it appears impossible, unless there is some other route. Once the hero has begun his initiatory journey, there is no returning to a state of innocence.[8]

Second, the clashing gate is a motif resembling the Wandering Rocks, in Greek mythology located near the entrance to Hades. Odysseus is warned against them and decides to go another way (*Od.*, XII, 56ff.); only Jason, on his way to capture the Golden Fleece, has ever passed through safely. "The passage between the two rocks is clearly conceived as a gateway to another world . . . a door only momentarily opened . . . through [which] the . . . hero passes in the twinkling of an eye."[8] Compare the entrance into Moria—"They were just in time" (p. 322). The same motif appears alternatively in ancient art as a gap between two mountains, the single world navel having been doubled although (in the words of Heraclitus) the way up and the way down are really the same. It is this doubled version which provides Odysseus's alternative to the clashing rocks. He must make his way between a high peak inhabited by a man-devouring goddess (Scylla) and a lower mountain, an arrow's shot away, beside which is a powerful whirlpool (Charybdis) that would suck his ship down to the depths of the sea. Clearly Charybdis is yet another route to hell. Odysseus, who has already been there—Circe calls him "rash . . . /Dying twice, when other men die a single time" (XII, 21–22)— escapes Charybdis, though she claims his ship and his men. In Tolkien's version there are three mountains (but one, Fanuidhol, is unimportant). Like Odysseus, who risked the terrors of Scylla but then had to go by Charybdis anyway, the company tries to go over the Misty Mountains by the pass of Caradhras but ends up plunging into the depths under Mount Celebdil.

Immediately all is dark. To understand the significance of this fact in the experience of Moria, it is necessary to appreciate the numinous quality of utter darkness. In her Michigan dissertation on Tolkien ('The Structure of *The Lord of the Rings*', 1965, p. 102) Dorothy K. Barber has given this account:

> Especially for the urban person, it is increasingly difficult to experience complete darkness, but, like thousands of other tourists, I have experienced this once in the Cave of the Winds in South Dakota. The effects were unexpected. In a chamber where the turnings of the cave had cut off all natural light, the guide told the group he would turn out the electric light for just one minute. Comparing our feelings after this very long minute, we found we had all been afraid to move; we felt there was no ground around us, even though we all knew the chamber had a solid, even rock floor. Everyone had reached out to touch his companions, for each had felt utterly alone, cold and very anxious. We felt certain our eyes would never become adjusted to this darkness, as they do, in a slight degree, to the darkness of a moonless night. No one was in favor of repeating the experience.

From the sense of loneliness described here and the sense of the total irrelevance of all previously acquired knowledge as a guide in this new experience, we may see how naturally darkness symbolizes death and the journey to hell.

KNOWLEDGE AND SELF-KNOWLEDGE

The journey to hell serves two quite different functions in mythology. It may be the setting for the hero's most difficult struggle and greatest heroic feats, as in the case of Orpheus, Heracles, Beowulf beneath the mere, and Christ. But its main role may be to prepare the hero as he develops strength of character or gains information needed for the heroic deeds he is destined to perform. Aeneas's descent and Beowulf's swimming match with Breca are two examples, and there are several instances also in the Arthurian romances.[10] The descent into the underworld, or into the womb of Mother Earth, is also prominent in the initiation rituals of many cultures, including Christian baptism.[11] Some of these rituals represent a symbolic uniting of the two functions: the initiate is prepared for the tasks of life not only by instruction but by vicarious or sacramental participation in the triumphs of the archetypical hero.

For the hobbits the entire journey from the Shire to the East and back again is an initiation. They leave as children and return as tried warriors, mature in judgment and firm in resolve.[12] But what part of this change is accomplished specifically in Moria? One lesson they learn explicitly—"let the guide go first" (I, p. 326). Another is nearly as plain—don't idly throw rocks into pools or wells. But these things are trivial. Pippin learns courage when he must leap a seven-foot chasm, while the water below is sending up a grinding noise (p. 325). Frodo learns the value of Bilbo's gifts, the mithril coat and the sword Sting, as he earns Gandalf's praise, "There is more about you than meets the eye" (pp. 324, 339, 342). They all learn respect for the secrets hidden in the depths of Mother Earth and respect mingled with pity for the last days of Balin and his followers. After Gandalf falls, they learn to press on in the midst of sorrow and without hope until "at last, they came beyond hope under the sky and felt the wind on their faces" (p. 346). This is a valuable lesson, for now, says Aragorn, "we must do without hope" (p. 347).

Through his experience in Moria, Frodo gains in self-knowledge. He emerges with a confirmed sense of being protected for a mighty destiny by powers beyond himself. After

Moria he grows in responsibility until he is able to ascend the mountain alone, look at the choices before him and make his own decision to separate from the company and bear his burden without their aid. In Moria also he becomes aware for the first time of the presence of his *alter ego*, Gollum. Those furtive footsteps and pinpoint eyes represent Frodo's own desire to be invisible—a necessity, he thinks, in order to escape the Eye of Sauron. Actually invisibility is an evil to which the Ring is tempting him and which could reveal him to the Enemy (as it did on Weathertop). Throughout the work it is assumed that the peculiar origin of the Ring makes its use both dangerous and self-defeating. This is not arbitrary, but profoundly moral. The Ring offers the temptation to see without being seen, to know without being known. It is thus the aggressive side of sexuality isolated from the whole—possession without love, pure self-aggrandizement.[13] As such it is part of the psyche of every man and must become acknowledged if one is to progress to full maturity—it is not accidental that caves and labyrinths have a sexual symbolism and that finding one's way in a maze is an initiation suitable to coming-of-age.[14]

In any case, it is this aggressive part of Frodo which the fallen hobbit Gollum represents. On the long trek to Mordor, Sam begins to realize their kinship. Frodo and Gollum are bound together right to the end, until Gollum's death finally pays vicariously for Frodo's sin of arrogance. When Frodo looks at Gollum, he "can . . . see 'himself', struggling to stay alive against powers insuperably great."[15] It is fitting that this relationship should have its dim beginnings in the labyrinth of Moria.

WRESTLING WITH THE MONSTER

The other meaning of descent into hell—struggle and triumph—is associated in Moria with Gandalf. Moria houses not only inert obstacles but active monsters, orcs,[16] cave trolls, and a Balrog of Morgoth. This evil being can scarcely be described, save in similes. It is "something dark as a cloud" (I, p. 341); it is "a thing of slime, stronger than a strangling snake" (II, p. 105); it is "like a great shadow, in the middle of which was a dark form, of man-shape maybe" but of "great height" and wingspread, fire-breathing and with a blazing mane (I, pp. 344f.). It afflicts Legolas and Gimli with no ordinary fear but a totally enervating dread. The vagueness does not prove a lack of descriptive power on Tolkien's part but rather a sense of supernatural, unfathomable evil. Yet we are given enough details to perceive that the Balrog is a fitting adversary for Gandalf: "I have met my match" (p. 340). Both go back to the time before the Third Age. Both can "see" through doors, and know spells of great power. Both have the power of fire: Gandalf is "a servant of the Secret Fire, wielder of the flame of Anor" (the sun), but the Balrog possesses "the dark fire" and wields (or is?) the "flame of Udûn" (p. 344). This fire may be quenched, but the Balrog has power to rekindle it. He dwells in an "abyss" deep "beyond light and knowledge," "far under the living earth" at the "uttermost foundations of stone," a place of deep water that is "cold . . . as the tide of death" (II, p. 105). Clearly the Balrog, a servant of Morgoth from the First Age,[17] is the master of this underworld.

The story of Gandalf's struggle with him has many parallels in the myths of the hero overcoming a monster of 'the deep'. The water motif and the hand-to-hand combat remind us of Beowulf, the association with death brings to mind Christ's Harrowing of Hell,[18] and the ambiguous "man-shape" suggests Theseus's conquest of the Minotaur. Gandalf's friends' despair over his fate is paralleled in all three myths. I am not proposing specific sources for Tolkien's trilogy; the point is, rather, that he has skillfully woven together a whole array of motifs traditionally associated with this monomyth and has done it in a manner that reinforces basic structural patterns in his own work of art. To escape from the depths, Gandalf must rely on the Balrog's knowledge of "secret ways" and, grasping the monster's heel, is as indissolubly linked in fate to his enemy as Frodo is to Gollum.[19] The Balrog becomes Gandalf's Ariadne (as Gollum in *The Hobbit* was Bilbo's), bringing him out of the maze and up the Endless Stair. "From the lowest dungeon to the highest peak it climbed . . . in unbroken spiral . . . until it issued at last in Durin's Tower carved in the living rock. . . ." A tower atop a mountain, threaded vertically by a spiral passage that reaches down to the earth's center—clearly we are at the *axis mundi,* the still point of the turning world. Here, shrouded from the sight of men below, witnessed only by the sun, the mortal struggle of good and evil is enacted amid thunder, lightning, and smoke. Each assailant takes the other's life. The Balrog "fell from the high place and broke the mountain-side where he smote it in his ruin" (II, p. 106). The imagery reminds us of the fall of Lucifer (Isaiah xiv. 12ff.). But Gandalf too has gone into timeless darkness. Tolkien's language in the *Chronology* is plain. Gandalf "passes away. His body lies on the peak." Then he "returns to life" (III, p. 373), but in a resurrection body (to use the obviously relevant theological term) which is "light as a swan's feather" (II, p. 106). His rescue by the eagle, the divine bird, is one final image of ascent.[20]

The rest of the company meanwhile has gone on to Lothlórien. As with Candide and Cacambo in South America, a terrifying journey through narrow ways brings them by a secret entrance to an almost inaccessible legendary land—the terrestrial paradise of mythology.[21] The proximity of Lórien to Moria reinforces our observation that this region in Middle-earth is a world navel, touching the depths and the heights of experience. Here too we have an underground journey of sorts. The leaves overhead are so thick that all paths are in deep shade, and travelers go blindfolded as well. Lórien is a "Hidden Land . . . out of the world of this Sun, and few of old came thence unchanged" (II, p. 275). When the travelers leave, the moon is in the same phase as it was when they entered (the same is true for Gandalf's fall from the bridge and his return to life), underscoring the otherworldliness of this region and the events that take place there where time seems to stand still.

THE LANDSCAPE OF HELL

Thus far we have observed aspects of hell in several of Frodo's adventures. But seen as a whole his trek to Mordor is a journey to hell of the second type involving mortal struggle and victory for the sake of others. Mordor is the "black land" (Elvish), inhabited by the Dark Lord. Though not underground, it is as effectively secluded from the world by its wall of mountains and closely guarded passages. The main entrance, the Black Gate, is set in the "mouth" of the "Haunted Pass" and guarded by "Teeth" (II, p. 244). Within is Mount Doom (note the English associations of its other name, Orod*ruin*), a volcano whose fire is hotter than the hottest forge, for the Ring that can go through ordinary fire and remain cool to the touch can only be destroyed there. Not far away is the Dark Tower, a place of torture, and (except Gollum) "those who pass the gates of Barad-dûr do not return" (III, p. 309).

Once across the Great River, the way to Mordor—the "way down inside," as Gollum calls it (II, p. 227)—is a wasteland. First there are barren hills, then "livid festering marshes where nothing moved and not even a bird was to be seen" (p. 209) and where "mists curled and smoked from dark and noisome pools" (p. 232). The imagery of hell is abundant.[22] In the part known as the Dead Marshes there peer up beckoningly the faces of battle-slain, whose transition from life to the realm of death is gradual and prolonged. Beyond that is a region

> more loathsome far. . . . Even to the Mere of Dead Faces some haggard phantom of green spring would come, but here neither spring nor summer would ever come again. Here nothing lived, not even the leprous growths that feed on rottenness. The gasping pools were choked with ash and crawling muds, sickly white and grey, as if the mountains had vomited the filth of their entrails upon the lands about. High mounds of crushed and powdered rock, great cones of earth fire-blasted and poison-stained, stood like an obscene graveyard in endless rows, slowly revealed in the reluctant light. (p. 239)

This passage describes a familiar poetic landscape; we have encountered it in Browning's *Childe Roland* and Eliot's *Waste Land*. It bespeaks the sterility of a being who can at best counterfeit, not create (p. 89), and who prefers to destroy. It is enough to "unman" the soldiery of Gondor and Rohan (III, p. 162). Finally, approaching the pass into Mordor, there lie about the mouth itself "great heaps and hills of slag and broken rock and blasted earth, the vomit of the maggot-folk of Mordor" (p. 163). And this part of Frodo's journey to hell is not a matter of landscape alone but of the Ring which weighs more and more heavily on him and, still worse, of the growing power of the Eye.

Inside Mordor it is much the same: "ashes, and dust, and thirst . . . and pits" (II, p. 222). Every one of these words from Gollum's description is traditionally associated with death and hell. As the travelers approach Mount Doom, thirst is especially oppressive. Orodruin itself is a cone, a volcano, having in its side near the top a "dark door," a "gaping mouth" leading in to the Chambers of Fire (III, p. 222). This is at last the very center, the mouth of the innermost hell.[23] Frodo goes in. Sam follows in a "stifling dark" that even the phial of Galadriel cannot relieve. "He was come to the heart of the realm of Sauron and the forges of his ancient might, greatest in Middle-earth; all other powers were here subdued." And now the quest is over. With the help of his "other self" at the last, Frodo destroys the Ring and thus overcomes the lord of hell. The fire and smoke which marked Sauron's works are converted into psychological images of his own wrath and fear which "consume" and "choke" him (p. 223). Destruction overtakes the land of destruction, the underworld of Sauron falls before infernal forces. Twice before upon Frodo's emergence from a particular hell (Moria, Cirith Ungol) part of it was destroyed; this time, all of it is destroyed. Frodo and Sam themselves barely escape the volcanic eruption. Once again it is the eagles that perform the rescue.

Meanwhile, several others in the story have faced hells of their own, especially Aragorn who, like Frodo in the Dead Marshes, must confront the twilight kingdom between death and life. He undertakes this necessary journey in response to an oracular call and against his own inclinations (III, p. 48). It may be his "doom . . . to tread strange paths that others dare not" (p. 52), but the decision is not reached without a "bitter struggle" (p. 53)—no Gethsemane of submission but a confirmation of mastery through the Stone of Orthanc. The Paths of the Dead are a way of terror, haunted by the "forgotten people" whose curse forbids them to know peace until their oath to fight Sauron is fulfilled. Ancient sculptures stand "like rows of old and hungry teeth" (p. 68) guarding the road to the "forbidden door." But Aragorn's sense that his destiny leads this way is confirmed by the fact that the great army of the Sleepless Dead has begun to assemble "as if . . . to keep a tryst" (p. 70). Whispering, they throng after the Grey Company as it passes along the way in darkness and extinguish the company's torches with a "chill blast" (pp. 60f.). In the world outside it is day, but their way goes through a canyon so deep that stars shine. "It might have been twilight in some later year, or in some other world." Thus the pattern that we have noted for Frodo and Gandalf is repeated for Aragorn—an adventure that is explicitly otherworldly. The Cosmic Pillar is part of this pattern too: the summons of the Oathbreakers out of their "grey twilight" occurs at a huge spherical black stone ("unearthly it looked, as though it had fallen from the sky"), a relic of the

Númenorean realm of old (p. 62). Holding this terrifying host to obey his commands, Aragorn proves his credentials as king, though he will again be called on to prove them in the Houses of Healing.

To Éowyn, Aragorn in his determination to go by the forbidden way seemed "fey . . . , and like one whom the Dead call" (p. 71). *Fey* is a word that Tolkien applies to several others as well. Others besides Aragorn seem to be seeking death; it is a theme prominent in the story while the darkness is over Gondor. Théoden may criticize Aragorn for taking the Paths of the Dead, yet his actions reflect the same attitude. He thinks of the journey to Gondor as one leading to death. "There may be other roads than one [The Paths of the Dead] that could bear that name" (p. 73). And as he led his army into battle (p. 112) "fey he seemed." So too Éowyn, alias Dernhelm, displays "the face of one without hope who goes in search of death" (p. 76). Later, thinking his king and sister both dead, Éomer is seized by a "fey mood" and leads the Rohirrim with the battle cry of *Death* (p. 119), though soon his mind will become "clear again" (p. 122). Denethor in the Tombs is "fey and dangerous" (p. 101); Frodo running though the tunnels after the first encounter with Shelob is "in a fey mood" (II, p. 334). The word suggests possession by spirits, the opening of the mind to forces from a different world.

An important question should be raised at this juncture: Is there a distinction between otherworlds? Are some of these fey moods celestial, others diabolical? Aragorn acts deliberately, on reliable messages and impulses, but the others all seem, at least to some degree, under the influence of the Darkness. And in the Houses of Healing it is Aragorn who counters that influence, venturing once again into the twilight kingdom. "Aragorn's face grew grey with weariness, and ever and anon he called the name of Faramir, but each time more faintly to their hearing, as if Aragorn himself was removed from them, and walked afar in some dark vale, calling for one that was lost" (III, p. 141). Then to Éowyn also he goes, "to recall her from the dark valley" (p. 143). By using *athelas*, an herb from Númenor, to cure the Black Breath, he pits the 'celestial' otherworld directly against the infernal. Its "fragrance . . . was like a memory of dewy mornings of unshadowed sun in some land of which the fair world in Spring is itself but a fleeting memory" (p. 142).

II. The Image of the City

The image of hell can be found in the creations of men as well
as in the natural world. In Genesis Cain was the first city builder.
Long after him the evil descendants of Noah said to one another,
"Come, let us build ourselves a city and a tower with its top in
the heavens, and make a name for ourselves; or we shall be dis-
persed all over the earth" (Genesis xi. 4). The Tower of Babel
has come to stand for the endeavors of atheistic or rebellious
humanism. Yet the building of this tower was in its way a religious act—idolatrous to be sure, but not atheistic. "A tower with
its top in the heavens" would be designed to ensure unbroken
accessibility to the divine—an attempt to undo the expulsion
from Paradise. Babel, like its linguistic twin Babylon, means 'the
gate of God'. A city is, symbolically, an expression of man's
search for God whether seen horizontally or vertically—that is,
in the drawing together of crowds of people to live in harmony
or in the upward thrust of the temple on a hilltop. But it is
always a flawed expression: the earthly city can never be more
than an approximation of felicity.[24] Psalm 107 tells of a wandering people in search of their city. In Psalm 48 they have found
it: God himself is its tower, and "the joy of the whole earth is
Zion's hill." But the Epistle to the Hebrews finds in the wilderness wanderings a metaphor for the pilgrimage to heaven,
which is a city built by God.[25] Finally, in the Apocalypse (xxi.
2ff.) the true city comes down out of the heavens as the antithesis to Babylon, which has at last been destroyed. I have drawn
examples from the Bible, but they can be paralleled wherever
the myth of the earth navel is found—the sacred center, the axis
of Middle-earth.

The symbolic landscape of *The Lord of the Rings* is a wilderness dotted with centers of civilization, pinpoints of light in the
darkness. Except for Tom Bombadil's house and Rivendell,
which are single dwellings, there is in all of them an unusual
emphasis on the vertical. The villages of the Shire are generally
horizontal—arranged on the pattern of an ordinary English vil-
lage—yet even they go into the ground, and Michel Delving is
a "great digging." As the Ring goes south, the accent on vertical
structures increases: the ruined civilization of the dwarves under
the mountain; Caras Galadon aloft in the trees; Orthanc ('Mount
Fang') with its platform set amidst sharp pinnacles five hundred

feet above the plain, the mountain fortresses of Rohan, Minas Tirith and the procession of other towers on to the east. As long as the society has a wholesome element, its setting retains a horizontal dimension. In Minas Tirith the way in which outlying provinces and friendly kingdoms rally to the defense of the city demonstrates the achievement of Gondor in maintaining the principles of reciprocity and responsibility that make human society possible. On the other hand, the centers of evil are almost wholly vertical.

THE FOUR TOWERS

The title of *The Two Towers* refers to Minas Tirith and Barad-dûr, the rival fortresses in Frodo's vision from Amon Hen which closes the second of the six books (I, p. 417). Two other towers are also prominent in this volume, Orthanc and Cirith Ungol. Let us consider these four.

Minas Tirith (the 'Tower of Guard') is built like an ancient city of defense. Like Mordor it has its wall, and its strong gate. Inside one must go by labyrinthine ways to reach the Citadel seven hundred feet up and the White Tower, twice as high as Orthanc. A Stone of Seeing is kept in its upper chamber. Each of the seven levels of Minas Tirith has a wall and the entrances are staggered to make access difficult.[26] The pyramidal shape and the number of levels is also significant. Minas Tirith resembles a Babylonian ziggurat,[27] except that it is carved out of a mountain rather than built up from the plain. The "one white tree," now dead but renewed before the tale ends, is a link with Númenor in the West and completes the view of Minas Tirith as a place where earth and heaven meet.

Once again, however, the world's axis has its infernal as well as its celestial dimension. Minas Tirith is a great city, but it is dying.

> In every street they passed some great house or court over whose doors and arched gates were carved many fair letters of strange and ancient shapes: names Pippin guessed of great men and kindreds that had once dwelt there; and yet now they were silent, and no footstep rang on their wide pavements, nor voice was heard in their halls, nor any face looked out from door or empty window. (III, p. 24)

As in the city so in the heart of its ruler, death seeks ascendancy. In the chapter 'The Siege of Gondor' the images of hell are found in the city of the Sun—at its edges and at its center. "The first circle of the city is burning," is the news brought to Denethor in the White Tower. "Better to burn sooner than late," he replies, "for burn we must. . . . I will go now to my pyre." His son Faramir is "already burning . . . His house crumbles" (p. 98–99). The episode that follows in the narrow back passages of Minas Tirith is in its way as dreadful as anything in Moria. From the Citadel, Denethor goes "out into the darkness" (no normal darkness) and down to the Hallows, the houses of the dead, west of the city proper on what is called Silent Street. As the darkness begins to break outside and the cock crows, Denethor, within the House of the Stewards, is preparing the pyre to burn himself and his son alive. What Gandalf says to him is worth quoting here because it illustrates the emergence of hellish forces at the very point where earth meets heaven. "Authority is not given to you . . . to order the hour of your death. . . . Only the heathen kings"—one of the rare direct religious references in *The Lord of the Rings*—"under the domination of the Dark Power, did thus, slaying themselves in pride and despair, murdering their kin to ease their own death" (p. 129). A few lines later we learn that in fact Denethor, through the *palantír*, is also "under the domination of the Dark Power." He lights the pyre and leaps upon it, and the fire is so hot it causes the stone building to fall. This is truly the end of the Stewards' house, in both senses. A high and noble ideal, faithful stewardship for an absent lord, maintained for nearly a thousand years with little hope of the lord's return, collapses under the weight of pride and despair just as the hope is on the verge of being realized.

Faramir is rescued and taken to the Houses of Healing, located on the sixth level not far from the door leading down to the tombs. Meriadoc, on his way there after his encounter with the Black Rider, dreams he is in "a tunnel leading to a tomb; there we shall stay forever" (p. 134); but he too is saved. Life and death come near to one another in the greatest of Tolkien's cities.

The other towers are more deathly. The twin of Minas Tirith is Minas Morgul, now a dead city and seldom mentioned in the story. Farther east is the tower of Cirith Ungol, which together with the passage up to it through the mountains is the scene of perhaps the most terrifying of all Frodo's underground journeys. Again the physical setting has many of the symbolic attributes of the world's axis: mountain, tower, two stone guardians,[28] on the other side a winding stair coming up from the Morgul Valley, and a dark tunnel or cave inhabited by a monster who is the embodiment of evil. Moria was dark but this tunnel is worse. "Sound fell dead" in the heavy air, and the darkness blinded minds as well as eyes (II, p. 327). As sight and hearing are lost, smell becomes the dominant sense, only to add to the torment. "Here the return-to-the-womb is represented not by descent into an abyss and an underground sea, but by a loathsome female figure . . . the all-devouring Mother and vomiter of darkness."[29]

What there is of society in Cirith Ungol has never been held together by anything more than terror or violence. It is on the verge of collapse immediately after Frodo's encounter with Shelob, and as this part of the story resumes in the sixth book, we see society giving way to betrayal and murder. If the last of C.S. Lewis's *Screwtape Letters* (dedicated to Tolkien in 1942) is compared with some of the orc conversations (for instance III, pp. 202f.), it is clear that the principles holding Sauron's society together are those of hell (and the opposite of those of Minas Tirith).

There is something of society to be seen on the way across Mordor, but it bears no resemblance at all to the earthly city. A large camp of the assembling army is likened to an ant hill (p. 200); in the troop of soldiers that Sam and Frodo are forced to join for a while the only law is the whip.

But at least the uruks are capable of conversation. In the "cruel pinnacles" of Barad-dûr, the real counterpart to Minas Tirith, there is no one except Sauron with sufficient personal identity to be able to converse; and Sauron is known only by an Eye, a mind, a controlling will, and a Ring that has absorbed much of his strength (III, p. 219; I, p. 267). His lieutenant once had a name but is now just the Mouth of Sauron. The ring-wraiths are merely "slaves of the Nine Rings" (III, p. 364).

Yet by some measurements Mordor could be called a great nation. Barad-dûr itself is described as a "vast fortress, armoury, prison, furnace of great power" (II, p. 161). To run such an operation takes people and organization. Besides a huge army, Mordor has agriculture ("the great slave-worked fields away south," [III, p. 201]), commerce ("long waggon-trains of goods and booty and fresh slaves"), industry ("mines and forges" in the north), and a vast intelligence network of secret agents. Its landscape of pits and slagheaps and polluted waters is the typical countryside for a region of heavy industry. It is true that Sauron has no use for beauty or for living things that are merely neutral; further, he "can torture and destroy the very hills" (I, p. 279). Still, he is not utterly without creative accomplishment. He learned how to breed trolls that could endure the sun (III, p. 410) and brought the elven smiths to "the height of their skill" (p. 364). It was Sauron himself who forged the One Ring. (For such achievements today one might at least be rewarded with a professorship.)

We are getting into the question of Tolkien's attitude toward the values implicit in different kinds of social organization and economic systems. That attitude is more complex than we might be tempted to think at first. Let us look at one or two more examples.

Saruman's tower, nearly as tall as the Washington Monument, stood in a plain a mile in breadth ringed by a high wall. Beyond the wall, apart from a few acres tilled by Saruman's slaves, grass and groves had given way to brambles and burnt stumps. A long tunnel guarded by heavy iron gates led through the black wall into this industrial hell. The plain surrounding Orthanc, once a garden, now consisted of stone roads lined with chains, converging on the tower like spokes of a wheel, and between the roads were

> chambers . . . cut and *tunnelled* back into the walls upon their inner side, so that all the open *circle* was overlooked by countless windows and *dark* doors. . . . The plain, too, was bored and delved. Shafts were driven *deep* into the ground; their upper ends were covered by low *mounds* and domes of stone, so that in the moonlight the Ring of Isengard looked like *a graveyard of unquiet dead.* For *the ground trembled.* The shafts ran down by many slopes and *spiral stairs* to *caverns* far under; there Saruman had *treasuries,* store-houses, armouries, smithies, and great *furnaces. Iron wheels* revolved there *endlessly,* and hammers thudded. At night plumes of vapour steamed from the vents, *lit from beneath* with red light, or blue, or *venomous* green. (II, p. 160; italics mine)

The imagery is familiar, its connotations plain. This is yet another hell.

TECHNOLOGY, THE PRECIOUS BANE

One cannot help admiring the tower itself, however. It is "of marvellous shape . . . fashioned by the builders of old . . . a strong place and wonderful" (p. 160). It resists all the ents' attacks. Once again we face the ambiguity of the works of man. Call it technology or craftsmanship, it may be (Tolkien seems to be saying) neither wholeheartedly embraced nor utterly rejected.

The contrast between the industrial and the pastoral is made explicit in Isengard's fate. The moving trees compress into a few moments what would normally be done irresistibly by root systems over a span of years: the dead underground of Saruman's city is ruined by underground life. Both life and death here are underground.

Saruman's factories are wrecked, their fires put out, the land irrigated and gardens and orchards restored. We recall Legolas's plans for Minas Tirith. "The houses are dead, and there is too little here that grows and is glad. If Aragorn comes into his own, the people of the Wood shall bring him birds that sing and trees that do not die" (III, p. 148). Again, however, the works of man are set alongside rather than against the works of nature. Gimli the dwarf criticizes the stonework of the city. "When Aragorn comes into his own, I shall offer him the service of stonewrights of the Mountain, and we will make this a town to be proud of."

Dwarfs were the craftsmen of Norse mythology. In Tolkien's Middle-earth some very expert work is done by Elves (the Three Rings, the sword Glamdring) and Men (stonework in the mountains above Rohan), but outside of Sauron's realm it is the dwarves who are primarily associated with technology. Let us go back to their most extensive mines, about which Galadriel says, "Fair were the many-pillared halls of Khazad-dûm in Elder Days before the fall of mighty kings beneath the stone" (I, p. 371). There was a great civilization in Moria, and at other centers; they were great not only in wealth or material achievement but in culture, loyalty, and endurance. Consider for example Gimli's capacity for appreciating the beauty of the caves of Helm's Deep and his eloquence in describing them:

immeasurable halls, filled with an everlasting music of water that
tinkles into pools, as fair as Kheled-zâram in the starlight. . . . Gems
and crystals and veins of precious ore glint in the polished walls;
and the light glows through folded marbles, shell-like, translucent
as the living hands of Queen Galadriel. There are columns of white
and saffron and dawn-rose. . . .

It goes on, line after line (II, pp. 152f.). We are reminded of those
medieval tales where the approach to paradise is through a tunnel or cavern illuminated by the glitter of its own gems.[30] As the
tombs are not far from the Houses of Healing in Minas Tirith,
the underworld has its beauty and terror side by side.

It has terror because it is possible (through greed) to dig too
deep and unleash monstrous forces. The one mineral which is
Tolkien's invention, mithril, is valuable both for its beauty and
for its virtue as armor, but it is also a symbol for devastating
greed. Greed appears too in the Barrow-wights, whose spell is
broken by giving the treasure away. So also the dragon, not
only in *The Hobbit* but in *Beowulf* and throughout Germanic
folklore, is an emblem of the evil inherent in the mineral treasures hidden in the womb of Earth.[31] We are reminded too of
the satanic associations of mining and metalworking. *Paradise
Lost,* I, 670–751, conveniently collects for us the commonplaces
of tradition, some of them going back to classical writings relat-
ing the discovery of fire and the beginnings of mining and met-
allurgy to a fall from the Golden Age."[32] In Milton's epic a
group of fallen angels led by Mammon sets up a whole industrial complex in Hell for the building of Pandemonium. Some
mine gold from a hill "whose grisly top/Belched fire and rolling
smoke," others smelt the ore in furnaces dug into the plain
("many cells . . ./That underneath had veins of liquid fire/
Sluiced from the lake"), and others cast the molten gold in
molds and perform the various construction trades. Milton also
informs us that it was by Mammon's instruction that humans
later "Ransacked the center, and with impious hands/Rifled the
bowels of their mother earth/For treasures better hid." Gold is
a "precious bane" that is fittingly found in hell.

The oxymoron "precious bane" neatly poses the dilemma.
On the one hand, many primitive cultures revere the smith as a
person of divine power equaling or exceeding that of the
shaman and even as a descendant of the gods who entrusted

him with the secret of fire.[33] On the other hand, his powers are widely attributed to trafficking with the devil. This infernal aspect may take mythical form in the figure of the dwarf, who in Norse mythology was *draugr*, living dead, and belonged essentially to the lower world.[34] Medieval folklore recognized two archetypical masters of fire, Jesus and the devil.[35] (We may note a parallel in the confrontation of Gandalf and the Balrog in Tolkien's tale.) Prometheus's theft of fire for man has long been looked upon as an ambiguous gift.

The infernal side of technology is particularly evident in war. Another passage from Milton offers an interesting parallel to *The Lord of the Rings*, Satan's invention of artillery for the war in heaven. Digging in the "celestial soil," the rebel angels find minerals and stones to make cannons and shot, and "sulphurous and nitrous foam" from which "with subtle art" they make explosives; all suitable materials because "pregnant with infernal flame" (*Paradise Lost*, VI, 509–519, 483). Compare this with the siege of Gondor. The weapons of the defenders are essentially medieval ones—spears, swords, bows and arrows—but the hosts of Sauron use elaborate war machines manufactured in Mordor, a great hammer to batter down the gate and a new kind of catapult that firebombs the city.

These observations will aid in the analysis of Tolkien's moral vision. Along the vertical line which organizes his moral world, mobility predominates over rest. It is true there are some beings confirmed in evil, but even among them, figures such as Sauron and Morgoth seem to have become evil through rebellion at some remote time. With their opposites in the tale, Gandalf and Galadriel, the situation is different. To refer to them as confirmed in goodness makes sense only if the phrase permits the ever-present possibility of their fall. Tolkien makes this point clear by having each one face temptation to take the Ring and *not immediately* overcome it. In between these extremes lie the vast majority of Tolkien's men, elves, dwarves, ents, wizards, and hobbits. They are never at any time automatically good or automatically evil. Denethor, Saruman, Théoden, Frodo, Gollum—call the whole roll and the story is the same. They always possess the potential for good and evil, and every moment is one of decision.

This analysis of Tolkien's moral vision is reinforced by his treatment of the inanimate world that furnishes man with the opportunity and the challenge to be a subcreator. Objects are not in themselves good or evil, but nearly everything has a potential for both. Mithril is both the greatest of treasures and a deadly bane. Cities are built on an axis that reaches to hell as well as to heaven. (Our own ambivalent feelings toward the urban centers in America reflect essentially the same view.) Minas Tirith barely escapes falling, and not from external enemies alone, yet Isengard after the destruction of its war plants can be made into a garden again. Though Minas Morgul is razed by command, there is a hint that even it "may in time to come be made clean" (III, p. 247). The dual potential included in the capacity of "making" embraces poetry and jewelry as well as instruments of war and torture. The cave may be a place of glittering beauty as well as darkness. The mastery of fire produces bombs, but also comfortable hearths and homes.

This brings us back to the hobbit hole and perhaps to a line from one of Tolkien's poems: "Deep roots are not reached by the frost" (I, p. 182). The essential optimism of this line is quite in keeping with the nearly timeless perspective we find in *The Lord of the Rings:* more than sixty-five centuries of detailed chronology, receding into a First Age of unspecified duration and pointing ahead to a yet unknown future. (Will Shelob return? Will Morgul Vale and Orthanc ever be inhabited? Will ents find entings?) Not only is the future unknown, but to us (and to the Third Age) it is unknowable. As we have already seen—good and evil are not automatic, and potentially anything is possible. But with his perspective of millennia, Tolkien shows the triumphs and tribulations of history nearly *sub specie aeternitatis.* Despite immeasurable sorrow as well as joy, and despite the evils perpetrated by powers that at times may seem invincible,[36] he sees at the ultimate ending of the human story happiness—'eucatastrophe'. Events in Tolkien's trilogy happen by design, not chance. In a closed universe good and evil could only seesaw endlessly and meaninglessly, but in Middle-earth (a term unknown from pre-Christian English) hanging between heaven and hell, Tolkien sees hope.

NOTES TO CHAPTER 9

1. Helen Gardner, ed., *John Donne: The Divine Poems* (Oxford, 1952), Appendix F.

2. E.A.S. Butterworth, *The Tree at the Navel of the Earth* (Berlin, 1970), especially Chapter 1, Pl. 29, and p. 213, where the iconography of a medieval crucifix is traced to Asian and Minoan sources to demonstrate that the Cross is thought of as 'the cosmic tree'. See also Mircea Eliade, *Images and Symbols* (New York, 1961), pp. 39–51, and Joseph Campbell, *The Hero with a Thousand Faces,* Bollingen Series 17, second edition (Princeton, 1968), pp. 40–46. H.R. Patch collects numerous examples of these and other motifs in *The Other World* (Cambridge, Mass., 1950). Northrop Frye, *Fables of Identity* (New York, 1963) pp. 58ff., briefly traces the motif in literature.

3. *Paradise Lost,* IV, 269ff. See the discussion of this passage, and its echoes in *Kubla Khan,* in Maud Bodkin, *Archetypal Patterns in Poetry* (New York, 1958), pp. 87–94. On the hollow mountain see Patch, pp. 234n., 318.

4. Cf. Bodkin, pp. 100–06.

5. "There are some things that it is better to begin than to refuse, even though the end may be dark" (Aragorn). J.R.R. Tolkien, *The Two Towers* (London, 1954), p. 43. All references in this chapter to *The Lord of the Rings* will be to the original London edition in three volumes.

6. See Burton Stevenson, *The Home Book of Proverbs, Maxims, and Familiar Phrases* (New York, 1948), p. 524, for Hebrew, Greek, Latin, and English proverbs to this effect.

7. Note the parallels to some of these details in the lakes described by Patch, pp. 225, 265f., from medieval allegory and romance.

8. Once the initiatory secret has been whispered, once the ritual incision has been made, the former state cannot be restored. A parallel event occurs when the hobbits leave the womb-like Shire: the heavy gate "shut with a clang, and the lock clicked. The sound was ominous" (I, p. 121). But at that stage of their journey, the word "ominous" can convey only the smallest fraction of the terror induced by the gate-closing at Moria.

9. Butterworth, pp. 183–84. See also Mircea Eliade, *Birth and Rebirth* (New York, 1958), pp. 64–66, and Patch, p. 266 n. 112. Subsequent references to Eliade if not otherwise specified are to *Birth and Rebirth.*

10. Eliade, p. 125. "The very word [*initiation*] comes from a special use of the Latin word 'inire', 'enter', to signify 'ritual entry into the earth'" (W.F. Jackson Knight, *Vergil: Epic and Anthropology* [New York, 1967], p. 176). In the case of Browning's *Childe Roland,* the initiation

rite (note the significance of the title 'Childe') and the greatest possible feat of heroism turn out to be one and the same.

11. Eliade, pp. 51–52, 58, 61ff., 120.

12. Actually only Pippin had not yet 'come of age', but the characteristic existence of hobbits is childlike (size, love of parties and fireworks, ignorance of the outside world). See Marion Zimmer Bradley, 'Men, Halflings, and Hero Worship', in Neil D. Isaacs and Rose A. Zimbardo, eds., *Tolkien and the Critics* (South Bend: University of Notre Dame Press, 1968), pp. 109–127, and Hugh T. Keenan, 'The Appeal of *The Lord of the Rings:* A Struggle for Life', Isaacs and Zimbardo, pp. 67–70.

13. "The Ring is the ultimate danger because it embodies the final possessiveness, the ultimate in power that binds things apart from ourselves to ourselves." Roger Sale, 'Tolkien and Frodo Baggins', Isaacs and Zimbardo, p. 264.

14. The forty miles beneath Celebdil are laced with passages so unimaginably "intricate" and "bewildering" that even Gandalf must sometimes rely on intuition (I, pp. 324, 328). On the labyrinth as a common initatory test see Knight, pp. 266ff.; on the sexual symbolism, Knight, p. 180.

15. Sale, p. 273; see also p. 282.

16. The term suggests the Roman god of the underworld (J.S. Ryan, 'German Mythology Applied: The Extension of the Literary Folk Memory', *Folklore* 77 [1966], pp. 52–53). Ryan's article is heavily though silently indebted to Douglass Parker, 'Hwaet We Holbytla. . . ,' *Hudson Review* 9 (1956–57), pp. 598–609.

17. Jared C. Lobdell, 'A Medieval Probverb in *The Lord of the Rings*', in John L. Cutler and Lawrence S. Thompson, eds., *Studies in English and American Literature: American Notes and Queries Supplement, Volume 1* (Troy, NY, 1978), pp. 330–31.

18. See J.A. MacCulloch, *The Harrowing of Hell* (Edinburgh, 1930).

19. Thus "I have met my match" suggests (besides the obvious meaning) the 'other self', *alter ego, Doppelgänger.* For *match* in English two meanings grew up side by side, 'equal adversary' and 'marriage partner', or simply 'marriage'. A similar homophony has developed for English *mate* 'sexual partner' and (of separate origin) *mate* as in *checkmate.*

20. On the significance of the spiral stair cf. Eliade, p. 14; Dante's ascent of Mount Purgatory; Donald A. Mackenzie, *The Migration of Symbols* (New York, 1926, reprinted 1970), pp. 111ff.; and G.R. Levy, *The Gate of Horn* (London, 1948), pp. 136, 169f. "North" in the passage from Isaiah is the region of the Pole star, hence the *axis mundi,* or earth's axis. On eagles, see Butterworth, pp. 202–06, and consider

Tolkien's previous use of eagles to rescue Gandalf (I, p. 275) and in *The Hobbit*. Gracia Fay Ellwood, *Good News from Tolkien's Middle Earth* (Grand Rapids, 1970), pp. 113–18, develops some of these mythic motifs using Gandalf as a Christ figure.

21. A.H. Krappe, 'The Subterraneous Voyage', *Philological Quarterly* 20 (1941), pp. 119–130, traces this motif through medieval stories back to the *Epic of Gilgamesh*.

22. The swamps and the fortress-palace in the midst of Mordor are two striking parallels to a traditional near-eastern hell (Knight, p. 298).

23. Ellwood, p. 123, explains by the symbolism why Orodruin is the center and not Barad-dûr.

24. Charles Moorman, *The Precincts of Felicity* (Gainesville, 1966), pp. 6–7.

25. Hebrews xi. 10, 16; xii. 18–24; xiii. 14.

26. III, pp. 23–24. Knight, pp. 88ff., describes the same pattern in ancient cities and in labyrinth motifs in art.

27. Lest this seem a pointless parallel, let us remind ourselves of the amazingly tangled interpenetration of cultures. "The ziggurats affected Greek thought, for from them comes the belief in the soul's ascent to Heaven by way of seven circles, a belief which reached Dante by way of Spain from the Arabs . . ." (Knight, p. 221). Cf. especially Knight's description of the sacred city of Nippur, pp. 299f.

28. Cf. the clashing door motif again: "as plainly as if a bar of steel had snapped to behind him" (III, p. 179).

29. Ellwood, pp. 125–26. With Tolkien's presentation of Shelob, II, p. 133 ("who only desired death for all others . . .") cf. Milton's presentation of Death in *Paradise Lost*. Could the etymology of *Morgul* reflect those two deadly females in Arthurian myth, Morgan and Morgause?

30. Cf. Krappe, p. 123; and these lines from *Paradise Lost* (III, 608ff.): "with one virtuous touch/Th' arch-chemic sun, so far from us remote,/Produces, with terrestrial humor mixed,/Here in the dark so many precious things/Of color glorious and effect so rare."

31. See H.R. Ellis Davidson, 'The Hill of the Dragon', *Folklore* 61 (1950), pp. 178f.

32. For example Seneca, *Natural Questions*: "Avarice hath digged into the veins of the Earth and Rocks, seeking in darkness the ruin of Mankind." Quoted by K. Svendsen, *Milton and Science* (Cambridge, Mass., 1956), p. 121.

33. Mircea Eliade, *The Forge and the Crucible* (New York, 1962), pp. 79–95.

34. C.N. Gould, 'Dwarf-Names: A Study in Old Icelandic Religion', *PMLA* 44 (1929), p. 959.

35. Eliade, *The Forge and the Crucible*, pp. 106–07.

36.   Compare this observation by Tolkien's contemporary, Edwin Muir: "Even under dictatorships . . . people have a spring of happiness . . . from . . . an inexhaustible, hidden source. We have come to think so much of politics as colouring or overshadowing all our thoughts and feelings that it is easy for us to forget the truth, . . . that the impulses of the heart come of themselves, and that our most precious experience takes place, happily for us, in a universal, unchanging underground" (*Autobiography* [London, 1954], p. 236).

10

Aspects of the Paradisiacal in Tolkien's Work

U. MILO KAUFMANN

A famous quatrain of Omar Khayyam runs, in Fitzgerald's translation:

Ah Love! could you and I with Him conspire
To grasp this sorry Scheme of Things entire,
Would not we shatter it to bits—and then
Re-mould it nearer to the Heart's Desire![1]

The difficulty with this fantasy is the ambivalence of human desire. Our deepest and simplest wishes are strangely contradictory. We wish for the novelty and boundlessness of the eternally changing, yet we also wish for the stability and permanence of the perfected, the static. We wish for a loving penetration of all things, yet we also wish for those things to preserve their integrity as Other.

This strange complexity of our desire is displayed most clearly in the traditional pictures of Paradise. For our purposes here, I shall define paradise as ideal or sublime finitude, as opposed to some kind of infinitude. Paradise will refer not to heaven, but to a focal point of reality at the edge or center of the world. For this definition, both the Garden of Eden, and its historical opposite, the New Jerusalem, are paradises—that is, walled places within the earthly world achieved by a kind of purification. The artist, we may suppose, begins with the world as we know it, and arrives at the paradisiacal by subtracting undesirable elements, such as pain, and evolving the remainder to its fullness. It will be apparent that in these terms, paradise may well either refer to a present physical reality, as a lost garden of Eden, or to a present spiritual order of reality, accessible to the sensitive individual. I mentioned the pictures of paradise revealing the complexity of our desiring. We may conveniently summarize the two related but conflicting elements of desiring as the wish for the ideal product and the wish for the ideal process. To use other categories, man wishes for both the Garden and the Abyss to which the Garden is inevitably joined.

In what follows, I propose to bring these categories to bear on the two most prominent features of the paradisiacal in J.R.R. Tolkien's fiction. I regard these features as 1. his uncanny capacity for making us see ordinary objects and actions bursting with the value of wholeness and finality, and 2. his talent for creating intransigently mysterious landscape. In the first case, we see common things as ideal products, the sort of completed whole articles we would associate with paradise as the realm of ideal products. In the second case, we see the world as endlessly mysterious because of its grounding in incompleteness in the potentiality of the Abyss. I will not take the time to review the thousand and one illustrations of these two talents we could readily find in *The Lord of the Rings* or in *The Hobbit*. Rather, I shall quote at some length from a story in which Tolkien describes the pattern for paradise. Of course I refer to that charming tale, 'Leaf by Niggle'.

Niggle is an odd little man who must make a long trip which he really does not want to make at all. He is an artist after a fashion, not the kind of artist who can paint a whole tree to perfection, but one who is skillful at painting an individual leaf. In his workshop he has canvas stretched, and he works for months and years on this painting of a tree. He paints a few details here and there to his satisfaction. Meanwhile, his neighbor Parish, who is lame, and a rather irascible fellow, is constantly interrupting him with his problems. Niggle resents this because it seems he is not going to finish his picture before he has to make his trip. It develops, of course, that he doesn't get it done. He has to give up his canvas to patch the leaking roof of his neighbor, and then the dreaded summons comes and he goes off.

Niggle Finds His Tree

By this time, we realize that we are following an allegory of death and the afterlife: this trip which Niggle takes with his work undone is the trip of death, and he moves into a work-house which is purgatory. Eventually the moment comes when he is ready to move beyond purgatory. He learns that a train is ready to take him to his new place. He slips out of the work-house and blinks a little. The sun is very bright. He walks briskly downhill to the station. The Porter sees him, says "This way!" and points Niggle's way to the little train:

> One coach, and a small engine, both very bright, clean, and newly painted. It looked as if this was their first run. Even the track that lay in front of the engine looked new: the rails shone, the chairs were painted green, and the sleepers gave off a delicious smell of fresh tar in the warm sun. The coach was empty.

The train moves off in a deep cutting with high green banks and before long whistles and brakes to a stop.

> There was no station, and no signboard, only a flight of steps up the steep embankment. At the top of the steps there was a wicket-gate in a trim hedge. By the gate stood his bicycle; at least, it looked like his, and there was a yellow label tied to the bars with NIGGLE written on it in large black letters.

Niggle mounts his bicycle and rides downhill in the sunshine.

> Before long he found that the path on which he had started had disappeared, and the bicycle was rolling along over a marvellous turf. It was green and close; and yet he could see every blade distinctly. He seemed to remember having seen or dreamed of that sweep of grass somewhere or other.

The ground levels off, and then rises again as he anticipates, and then a green shadow comes between him and the sun. He looks up and falls from his bicycle.

> Before him stood the Tree, his Tree, finished. If you could say that of a tree that was alive, its leaves opening, its branches growing and bending in the wind that Niggle had so often felt or guessed,

and had so often failed to catch. He gazed at the Tree, and slowly he lifted his arms and opened them wide.

'It's a gift!' he said. He was referring to his art, and also to the result; but he was using the word quite literally.

He sees that all the leaves he had ever worked on are present on the tree, and many leaves he had just begun to imagine. Astonishing birds mating, hatching, growing, even as he watches; live in the tree. Beyond the tree he sees the forest and the mountains.

> After a time Niggle turned towards the Forest. Not because he was tired of the Tree, but he seemed to have got it all clear in his mind now, and was aware of it, and of its growth, even when he was not looking at it. As he walked away, he discovered an odd thing: the Forest, of course, was a distant Forest, yet he could approach it, even enter it, without it losing its particular charm. He had never before been able to walk into the distance without it turning into mere surroundings. It really added a considerable attraction to walking in the country, because, as you walked, new distances opened out; so that you now had double, treble, and quadruple distances, doubly, trebly, and quadruply enchanting. You could go on and on, and have a whole country in a garden, or in a picture (if you preferred to call it that). You could go on and on, but not perhaps for ever. There were the Mountains in the background.

Soon Niggle is joined by his old neighbor, Parish. They tire at their work together, and they develop a few aches and pains in their joints. They are given tonics. "Each bottle had the same label: a few drops to be taken in water from the Spring before resting. They found the Spring in the heart of the forest; only once before had Niggle imagined it, but he had never drawn it. Now he perceived that it was the source of the lake that glimmered, far away and the nourishment of all that grew in the country."[2]

Three things should support firm conclusions about the paradise pictured in this tale. The first thing I would note is that it is a realm of archetypal forms, something like Edmund Spenser's 'Garden of Adonis', where there are to be found the seeds of things vital to generation and regeneration in time. But what is distinctive about Tolkien's paradise is that it is a landscape to which human creativity had made an important contribution.

What Tolkien calls subcreation[3] has been as essential to the constitution of this world as primary creation. Presented in tantalizing brevity is a notion of a realm of produced ideal forms which is suggested both in a variety of Oriental and Occult teachings and in the Biblical injunction, "Lay up for yourselves treasures in Heaven."

The second noteworthy thing about Tolkien's paradise is the presence of an all-sustaining spring, in a forest which never loses its mystery. This spring (joining the landscape to the waters beneath) and the perpetually fresh and exciting forest are two vehicles of Tolkien's affirmation of the dependence of the paradisiacal upon the Abyss. Indeed, his total conception is transparently a wedding of the two ideas of perfection and potentiality. Recall his words about that landscape: "you could go on and on, and have a whole country in a garden, or in a picture. You could go on and on, but not perhaps for ever. There were the Mountains in the background." We are talking about a limited world subject to a limitless variety of artistic perceptions and emphases.

The Infinite Potential of the Ordinary

Now, reflect with me on an old story, the story of the garden of Eden. I believe that the single most important feature of the description of that Garden is in the mist that waters its vegetation. There was no rain in Paradise; a mist came up from the ground and irrigated the growing things. This mist, which has traditionally been described as a fountain or spring, is the eruption into the closed garden of the primordial deep, the watery reservoir, which in the ancient Babylonian and Semitic worldview underlay the whole world. The world, in fact, floated on this reservoir, and it percolated into the closed space of Eden much as water would spout through the hole in a boat. The mist is the link between the garden of static, ideal perfection and the ineffably rich store of quality and possibility which the Deep represented. It is likely that the Hebrew affirmed the Deep primarily as a reservoir of fertility, but I think it is the implicit guarantee of the endless enrichment of being—of the endless growth of persons and other creatures, of the endless renewal and incrementation of both earth and heaven (an idea hinted in that unforgettable phrase of St. John in the *Apocalypse* xxi: 1,

"I saw a new heaven and a new earth.") The Abyss supports the affirmation that things can change for the better in an infinite chaining of novelty to novelty.

This grounding of our world in the Deep has important implications for the commonplace. It means that we are obliged to see the most ordinary of objects as alive with promise, electric with possibilities. Such confidence licenses the human imagination in its inveterate tendency to fix the momentary object as the resting place of final significance, and this transformation of the ordinary is precisely what we find happening throughout Tolkien's fiction. This is true not only of objects, but also of persons. Every man in his fathomless promise is a potential hero. The heroics of Bilbo and Frodo are much to the point, and Tolkien's style tells the tale. I find his epic delineation of the affairs of Rohan and Gondor in Books II and III of *The Lord of the Rings* less fitting. The style is prostituted to dress up heroics which are not thematically central. The homespun heroics of the hobbits have Tolkien's heart in them, and they bear out the implications of our thesis for the appreciation of person. Even the commonest person—even a Halfling—can do anything, if the demand is laid on him.

Allow me to excerpt briefly the most relevant comments which Tolkien makes upon these matters in his essay 'On Fairy Stories'. You will note his concern to glorify the ordinary object, and his concern also to present to us the fathomless mystery of our world. He says at one point in the essay, "We should meet the centaur and the dragon and then perhaps suddenly behold, like the ancient shepherds, sheep, and dogs, and horses—and wolves. This recovery fairy stories help us to make" (pp. 51–52). He says further, "Recovery (which includes return and renewal of health) is a re-gaining—regaining of a clear view. Of all faces those of our familiars are the ones both most difficult to play fantastic tricks with, and most difficult really to see with fresh attention, perceiving their likeness and unlikeness: that they are faces, and yet unique faces. This triteness is really the penalty of 'appropriation': the things that are trite . . . are the things that we have appropriated, legally or mentally" (p. 52). The business of art is to help us to recover them in their uniqueness and their value. He says, again, "Actually, fairy-stories deal largely with simple or fundamental things, untouched by fantasy, but these simplicities are made all the more luminous by their setting. For the storymaker who allows himself to be 'free with' Nature can be her lover, not her slave. It was in fairy-stories"—and here he says something we all knew he had to say some place—"It was in fairy stories that I first divined the potency of the words, and the wonder of the things, such as stone, and wood, and iron; tree and grass; house and fire; bread and wine."[4] To put his statements in the context of the present argument, we might say that for Tolkien the "recovery" of the commonplace involves seeing it *sub specie paradisi*. This means apprehending both its ideal completeness and its fathomlessness, its infinite potential. In its realization, the commonplace article suggests the realm of ideal products, sublime products. But in the diversity of means which the artist is free to employ in subliming the commonplace in the limitless perfectibility of the world at large, we have indicated that other pole of human desiring, ideal process. Art completes the world, but the world is never finished. The Garden and the Deep forever validate each other.

Gollum's Promise-Keeping

Thus far I have concentrated attention on two positive dimensions of the paradisiacal in Tolkien's art and we have seen how they are related. Yet to be entirely honest, we should notice one ramification of the paradisiacal which in fact constitutes a flaw in the probability of *The Lord of the Rings*—namely the way Gollum the monster keeps his promises.

For Tolkien, certain conventions about promise-keeping apply in the realm of Faerie. I may be stretching a point to insist that these conventions are explicable in terms of paradise, but I think not. The naturalness of promise-keeping is the issue. Tolkien says about the tale of *The Frog King:* "the point of the story lies not in thinking that frogs are possible mates, but in the necessity of keeping promises, even those with intolerable consequences. That together with observing prohibitions runs through all of Fairy-land. This is one of the notes of the horns of Elfland, and not a dim note" ('On Fairy-Stories', p. 59). Apparently it is true of Elfland, as it is true of Eden, that a powerful natural morality obtains, with a profound respect for the sanctions. Tolkien's comment illuminates though it does not legitimize what I have always found distracting both in *The Hobbit* and *The Lord of the Rings*. Gollum, the villain, is incredi-

bly conscientious. On the long trip to Mordor, he passes up a
thousand opportunities to sabotage the whole mission, presumably because he has to keep his promise. He may be a slimy
critter from waters under the earth, but obviously he is no
Leviathan. Leviathan, you remember, was the monster that the
Hebrew imagination always associated with chaos and the sea,
and the book of Job puts very eloquently his essential nature as
a monster. In ironic questions, God taunts Job: "Can you draw
out Leviathan with a fishhook? . . . Will he make a covenant with
you?" (xli: 1, 4). No reader needed to be told that Leviathan
would not make a covenant, for this is the critical distinction
between Nature and God. Nature did not keep its promises. In
the short term it might, but for the long haul, nothing less than
the promise of God sufficed. It is significant that after the great
Flood, God put a rainbow in the sky as witness to his promise,
not Nature's, that the regularities of seed-time and harvest, hot
and cold, would not thereafter be breached. And even this
covenant did not remove the mystery, the uncertain element
from Nature. It was God in whom one put his trust, not
Leviathan.

Leviathan is one thing, and Gollum is another: Gollum is
bound by promises. I shall leave you to reflect on whether or
not there is improbability here. I can only register the response
I felt when Frodo swore in Gollum as a guide for the journey to
Mordor. He should be put in chains. Frodo's confidence was—
there is no other word for it—childish. But of such is the kingdom of heaven.

Bombadil, the Power for Good in Nature

Finally, I should like to relate what I have been saying to the
enigmatic figure of Tom Bombadil, a nature sprite who appears
in the first volume. Tom is instrumental in freeing the wayfar-
ers from imprisonment in a cemetery by the infamous Barrow-
wights. The power that Tom Bombadil displays is so impressive
that the reader fears for a time that he will destroy the whole
fiction as a kind of universal solvent. Tolkien later makes a
point of meeting this threat. In the Council of Elrond, near the
close of *The Fellowship of the Ring*, the elves raise the question,
Why does not the plenipotent Bombadil take over the responsibility for destroying the Ring which Sauron seeks? The wizard

Gandalf replies: "No He might do so [take the Ring] if all the free folk of the world begged him, but he would not understand the need, and if he were given the Ring, he would very soon forget it, or most likely, throw it away. Such things have no hold on his mind. He would be a most unsafe guardian, and that alone is answer enough." Glorfindel the elf continues: "Could that power of Sauron be defied by Bombadil alone? I think not. I think that in the end, if all else is conquered, Bombadil will fall, Last as he was First, and then Night will come." Another elf adds: "Glorfindel I think is right. Power to defy our Enemy is not in him, unless such power is in the earth itself; and yet we see that Sauron can torture and destroy the very hills" (I, p. 348).

From these remarks, it appears that Bombadil represents the blind grace resident in Nature, a grace inferior to that made accessible to the obedient wayfarer. Bombadil is in two ways similar to the mysterious Melchizedek of *Genesis*. Melchizedek, you remember, was without known beginning of days, and he exercised extraordinary power over a natural realm, so much so that even Abraham was subservient to him. But Abraham, like the hobbits, goes on a pilgrimage in the context of a covenant which both demands and supplies more grace than Melchizedek can furnish.

We might say that Bombadil is the sum total of the power for good in Nature; hence he represents not only the good in any particular nature, but all that in the Abyss is capable of renewing Nature, capable of producing new natures. And standing beyond and subordinating that dread potency which, we are told, is not equal to the power of Evil—standing beyond Bombadil, beyond the power of Nature and the Abyss—is the divine potency available in covenant, which allows man to assume full moral stature and heroic dignity, manifesting his own transcendence of Nature.

Reaching beyond Nature for the power to overcome evil indicates not only Tolkien's theism but also his reservations about finitude, even about the sublime version called paradise. There is, to paraphrase Matthew Arnold, a power not ourselves, not even Nature's, which makes for righteousness. And to quote Wordsworth, "Our destiny, our being's heart and home, is with infinitude, and only there"[5]—that is, it lies beyond the mountains which rim Niggle's and every other paradise.

NOTES TO CHAPTER 10

1. Stanza 99 of *The Rubaiyat of Omar Khayyam* from James Stephens, Edwin L. Beck, and Royall H. Snow, eds., *Victorian and Later English Poets* (New York, 1949), p. 911.

2. 'Leaf by Niggle', in *Tree and Leaf* (London, 1964), pp. 84–88.

3. Cf. 'On Fairy-Stories', in *Tree and Leaf*, pp. 44–45.

4. P. 53. The essayist E.B. White has a little tale entitled 'The Second Tree from the Corner' which can profitably be compared with 'Leaf by Niggle'. The 'recovery' of a Tree in its perfection figures prominently in both.

5. *The Prelude*, Book 6, lines 604–05, in Thomas Hutchinson and the Reverend Ernest de Selincourt, eds., *The Poetical Works of Wordsworth* (London, 1936), p. 535.

Postscript

Twenty-eight years ago—it was the year after Ronald Tolkien's death—the first edition of this book was ready for the press. The world has changed since then, and the authors of the pieces included here have gone their separate ways. I believe all but one or two are still alive, though I am in touch with only a few. What the ways they have gone make clear is that this was the work of amateurs, in the best sense of that word. The authors were professional scholars with a love of Tolkien's books, but they were not professional Tolkien scholars. They were applying what they knew from their study in other realms to the realms of Middle-earth. In that was their strength, and in that remains the strength of these essays.

When I knew her in the 1970s, Bonniejean Christensen was a student of rhetoric, with a desire to study for the priesthood in the Episcopal Church. She was co-author, with Francis Christensen, of a book just coming out, *A New Rhetoric* (1976, second edn., 1978). Dorothy Matthews, at the University of Illinois, was not a scholar in any of the fields usually associated with Tolkien—Medieval Studies, for example, or Christianity and Literature, or even British Literature. In fact, I think I recall a study of Kate Chopin, perhaps somewhat later on. Walter Scheps, then at Ohio State, has since retired as Associate Professor at the State University of New York at Stony Brook. His expertise lay in Chaucer, still more in the so-called Scottish

Chaucerians, particularly William Dunbar: he published his volume on the *Middle Scots Poets* in 1986. Agnes Perkins established the Children's Literature program at Eastern Michigan University: in the 1990s she edited volumes I and II of the *Phoenix Award of the Children's Literature Association* (1993 for 1985–89 and 1996 for 1990–94). She and Helen Hill are, I believe, still in Ypsilanti: when this new edition was in the planning stages, she was in touch with Jan Finder, noting his success in mixing unmixable elements at the Conferences on Middle Earth (but I am not sure they were truly unmixable). Deborah Webster Rogers earned her Ph.D. from Wisconsin, settled in Des Moines with her husband, Ivor (who died this September), and they published their Twayne's English Authors volume on Tolkien in 1981. She gave a paper at the 1983 Marquette Conference on Tolkien, and has remained a gifted amateur in the field.

That year of 1981 saw the publication of three books on Tolkien by members of the University of Wisconsin Tolkien Society from the 1960s. Debbie's and Ivor's *J.R.R. Tolkien* (Twayne's) was one, my *England and Always* (Eerdmans) a second, and in that same year Richard West produced his *Annotated Check-List of Tolkien Criticism* (second edn.). Richard, represented here by what I still believe may be his best article, has also published a few other (very good) articles over the years, including 'Turin's *Ofermod*' in the recent Christopher Tolkien *Festschrift*. At the time he wrote the essay published in this volume he was a student of Arthurian Romance under the great Eugène Vinaver at the University of Wisconsin: he is still at Madison, but now and for many years as a principal librarian at the Kurt F. Wendt Engineering Library. David Miller remained a Professor of English at Purdue. Robert Plank, a generation older than the other scholars here, died in 1983: his last published work I recall seeing was a study of George Orwell, appearing (I think) in 1984.

Charles Huttar is Professor Emeritus of English at Hope College: with Peter Schackel he has edited collections of essays on C.S. Lewis (1990) and Charles Williams (1995), to both of which I contributed. U. Milo Kaufmann was already the author of *The Pilgrim's Progress and Traditions in Puritan Meditation* (Yale Studies in English 140, New Haven 1966). As a kind of follow-up, perhaps, to his study in this book, he published

'Paradise in the Age of Milton' in *ELS* in 1978. Now retired from the University of Illinois, he is active in the Free Methodist Church and was most recently co-author of *At Ease Discussing Money and Values in Small Groups* (1998) for the Alban Institute. Oh yes, and Jan Howard Finder, who put together the two Conferences on Middle-Earth is well-known in the circles of science-fiction fandom, is retired and living in Albany, and was Chairman of the 2001 Meeting of the Science Fiction Research Association there.

Rather a mixed bag, you might say, and you would be right, I suppose—but whether students of seventeenth-century litera-ture, or Medieval, or children's literature, or Kate Chopin, or George Orwell, rhetorician or psychoanalyst, all of us who con-tributed to this volume had one thing in common: *The Hobbit* and *The Lord of the Rings* (and 'Leaf by Niggle') were not part of our *workaday* world. They were not mine (I am by profession principally a teacher of economics and business, secondarily an editor, and occasionally a historian and a literary critic), and they were not the authors'—nor Jan Finder's, who created the Conferences on Middle-earth. We brought to our essays on Tolkien something of what Tolkien brought to his creation of Middle-earth, doing it for the love of it. I don't mean to imply that professional Tolkien scholars cannot make significant con-tributions to the field: they certainly can, and they do. I think particularly of the work of Professor Verlyn Flieger, who pre-serves much of the true amateur's enthusiasm in her profes-sional scholarship (which is of a very high degree). Nor do I mean that they do not love Tolkien. But I think (generally, even if not for Professor Flieger) that there may be a difference, at least between the *now* of 2002 and the *then* of 1969–73.

In 1987 I served as the Chairman of the Papers and Panels Committee for the Mythopoeic Society's Conference celebrating the 50th Anniversary of the Publication of *The Hobbit*, held at Marquette University in Milwaukee. We had ninety panelists and paper-givers (of an attendance of three hundred or so): half a dozen of them were contributors to this book. I noted then, and I have seen since, that there has been a kind of greying over of Tolkien scholarship. I don't mean that Tolkien scholars are get-ting older—greying in that sense—though obviously we are older now in 2002 than we were in 1974, or 1987, those of us who are still alive. I mean that the 'Frodo Lives' enthusiasm of the 1960s, the bright colors of the dawn in which it was bliss to be alive (and to be young was very heaven), the extramural love of 'Tolkien scholarship' in the fans who were also scholars (though not professionally of Tolkien), have all grown somewhat weaker, somewhat less bright. The scholarship has not, but I think the colors have.

It was bound to happen, of course. One recalls C.S. Lewis's remarks in *Screwtape*, about the falling away of enchantment that comes in the switch from reading the stories of the *Iliad* and *Odyssey* to buckling down and learning Greek. But that falling away of enchantment never came for Tolkien, and we do both ourselves and him better justice if it does not come to us in writing about his great book—or his other books. I have some quarrels with Peter Jackson's film version of *The Lord of the Rings* (at least in *The Fellowship of the Ring*, which is all I have yet seen)—why, for example, did he blunt the difference between Arwen and Eowyn by switching Glorfindel's ride with Frodo to Arwen? And why, particularly, did he give us in such detail the awfulness of the orcs? Nevertheless, I welcome the rebirth of enthusiasm it brings for Tolkien's world of the rings. Part of my own contribution to Tolkien study (beyond editing this volume) will appear shortly as *The World of the Rings* (being a revised and expanded version of 1981's *England and Always: Tolkien's World of the Rings*): here I am only an editor bringing the context of what I edited up to date. Thus, perhaps, very briefly, bringing up to date the story of Tolkien's scholar-fans, whose showcase this book was in 1974, and is still.

And perhaps I may be pardoned if I return to three of the points made in my original introduction, or implicit in the book. First, and most controversial at the time, I wrote that "if some of the authors misread Tolkien, at least it is quite clearly Tolkien they are misreading." To which one indignant reader pencilled in his margin, "Who else?" Well, most obviously, C.S. Lewis and Charles Williams, in particular, though mostly Lewis. To see Tolkien primarily as 'one of the Inklings' is not so much (in my view) inaccurate as it is limiting. I would suggest that the differences between—say—Lewis and Tolkien can be seen by looking at their antecessors and their successors.

Second, I wrote that "within the world of the Tolkien fans there is scholarship, high seriousness, and good writing." Though more 'fans' now than in 1974 are scholars *of* Tolkien—

that is, he is at least one of their academic specialties—I believe the high seriousness and (mostly) the good writing remain. That there is a loss in Tolkien's becoming an accepted subject of literary study in the academy I will not deny, but perhaps less than some others.

Third, at least implicit in this book as a whole, was and is my view that every reasonable engine of literary scholarship may reasonably be bought to bear on Tolkien's creation—that Tolkien criticism is part of literary criticism, and ought to involve some knowledge of the traditions of literature and the traditions of literary criticism. It ought not to be criticism *de novo*, as though *The Hobbit* and *The Lord of the Rings* were the first books ever written. There are, however, some difficulties here, in choosing the standards and the methods of literary criticism of *The Lord of the Rings*—and *The Hobbit* and *Farmer Giles of Ham* and *Mr. Bliss* and *Roverandom*, not to mention *The Silmarillion* and the whole *History of Middle-earth* put together by Christopher Tolkien.

Of course, the standards and methods of literary criticism are notoriously interwoven with the choice of a literary canon, and I should like to take the opportunity afforded me by this new edition to look briefly at Tolkien and English Criticism, going back to the *Defence of Poesie*, and the somewhat shamefaced admission by Sir Philip Sidney that his heart leapt up to hear the old ballad of Chevy Chase—because shamefaced, bearing witness to the strength of the sixteenth-century desire to reject the Medieval for the Classical, in literary model as in literary criticism. A rejection remaining pretty much in force until the Romantic Age ushered in—or was ushered in by—the Celtic and Medieval revivals.

There have been additional Medieval revivals since, of course. But attempts to make Professor Tolkien into a conscious standard-bearer for yet another Neo-Romantic attempt to restore the Medieval and reject the Neo-Classical (and its child, the Modern) would seem to fall afoul of one simple fact: he did not believe that what he was writing was reasonably the focus for literary criticism. To picture a group of 'Oxford Christians' planning to overthrow the Modern Age by meeting at the Eagle & Child or in C.S. Lewis's rooms at Magdalen, reading and talking to one another, is to misunderstand not only how things work, but the men and what they were doing. Indeed, far from wanting *The Lord of the Rings* as part of any canon—Medieval, Romantic, or otherwise—and thus a fit subject for literary criticism, Tolkien wanted to restrict the canon (if any) to the works of authors of ages gone by, and therefore restrict literary criticism to those works also. But the times, if you like, were against him, and what he did not intend to do, he did nonetheless. It is proper, I think, to ask: How did this happen?

The stream makes its own path, but the path it makes is determined by the force of the water and the shape and composition of the ground. John Ronald Reuel Tolkien was not constructing a *genre* predetermined by his critical views—not building a canal. His attitudes in and toward literary criticism are part of the story only as a clue to what he liked. And what he liked was what he wrote: the question is why what he wrote became what it did, a new *genre* to which is now generally given the name *fantasy*. This stream of Tolkienian fantasy begins in the medieval hills, the round hills of the English Midlands and the rocks and crags of the north and the Celtic outlands. From the medieval hills it flows in many channels, through the novels of Walter Scott (and his imitator Fenimore Cooper), as well as through the medievalist Pre-Raphaelites and their cousins the Nonsense writers.

The medieval consciousness of countryside grew into the Elizabethan Pastoral (for all its Classicist overlay), and pastoral grew into the song of the open roads of England and into the huntin'-shootin'-fishin' England of Surtees. Medieval carnival grew into the carnival of Victorian Christmas books and in humorists who trod the children's light fantastic. Medieval travel books of wonder, like Mandeville, were ancestor to Victorian 'thriller' writers like Stevenson and S.R. Crockett (and John Buchan), Henry Rider Haggard, and Arthur Conan Doyle. And late in the nineteenth century came those writers who calqued the world of the child on the form of pastoral, Kenneth Grahame and Rudyard Kipling—and, to some extent, G.A. Henty. Note that Crockett and Stevenson and Doyle and Kipling and Henty were historians of Great Britain.

This stream of literature is apart—often far apart—from the history of English Literature we have learned in our schools. And not only from the history of English Literature, but from literary criticism in English, and indeed in general. It has more to do with *The Gull's Horn Book* and *Kempe's Nine Days Wonder* than with Shakespeare, with Bunyan than with Milton, with *The Beggar's Opera* and even *Tom Jones* than with Swift or Pope or Johnson, with Surtees and early Dickens than with later Dickens and the other classic Victorian novelists, with the Nonsense writers and 'pop' fiction than with 'serious' literary artists—and above all with romance (in Harold Bloom's distinction) rather than with the novel. This is not to say that Tolkien's creation deliberately brought all these streams together, but there was indeed deliberation in his keeping apart from the stream at which literary critics have principally looked. The degree to which this deliberate keeping apart was tied to his view that 'current' English literature is not a thing to be studied in the schools—indeed, is a thing to be read rather than studied— is not certain, but the fact of the keeping apart is certainly related to the trouble critics may have had dealing with Tolkien's creation.

I suggest that, as pageant lies at the root of much science-fiction, so pilgrimage lies at the root of Tolkienian fantasy. Moreover, Tolkienian fantasy, in my view, is a version of pastoral. I believe pastoral can encompass both pageant—as with Lewis's interplanetary novels—and pilgrimage—as with *The Lord of the Rings*. But, of course (and this carries us back to the first point), there is a significant difference between pageant and pilgrimage, between Spenser (or Swift) and Bunyan, between Lewis and Tolkien. That is probably enough on this subject: it will be dealt with more fully in my forthcoming study on Tolkien and the origins of 'fantasy'. There is one more point I should mention here.

The first edition of this book included, as an Appendix, Professor Tolkien's guide to translators, 'Notes on the Nomenclature of *The Lord of the Rings*'. It was given to us for publication in *A Tolkien Compass*, and was indeed the first of his father's unpublished writings that Christopher Tolkien had edited and presented to the world. We had naturally expected to have it in this reprint, but it is now to be republished in another book through the Tolkien Estate, and the Estate has objected to its continued use in *A Tolkien Compass*—I suppose quite properly, though I wish it had been otherwise. We are thankful to have had the privilege of first bringing it out, as an Appendix to our original endeavor, and we remain grateful to Christopher Tolkien for its inclusion in the first edition—particularly since our version in proof required his substantial correction, which he graciously provided. In those days, of course, Christopher Tolkien was himself not known as the editor of his father's unpublished works, but as Reader in Icelandic Literature at New College, Oxford, and editor of *The Saga of King Heidrek the Wise*. In that, like us (though with far greater knowledge), he was an *amateur* of Tolkien, applying his professional knowledge and training to what he loved more.

As we were—and in this book, still are.

JARED LOBDELL
Elizabethtown, Pennsylvania
Michaelmas 2002

Index

Abraham (Biblical), 149
Abyss, 146, 149
    and paradise, 142, 145
Acton, Lord, 4
Adam (Biblical), 47, 72–73, 115
Aeneas, 119, 121
Aeneid, 119
Agamemnon, 106
Alice, 29
Alice's Adventures in Wonderland,
    28
Anborn, 46
Anduril, 72
anti-hero, in literature, 69
Aragorn, 45, 47, 49, 57, 70, 80, 82,
    84, 97, 119, 121
    as fey, 127
    as hero, 62, 71
    as king, 71-72, 73
    as Man, 67, 71
    nobility of, 64-65
    on Paths of the Dead, 125–26
Ariadne, 123
Aristotle, 52
Arkenstone, 38, 39
Arnold, Matthew, 149
Arthur, 28, 29, 103
Arwen, 72, 82
Auden, W.H., 2, 78

Baggins, Bilbo. *See* Bilbo
Baggins, Frodo. *See* Frodo
Balin, 121
Balrog, 43, 46, 96, 122–23
Barber, Dorothy K., 120
The Battle of Maldon, 78
Beorn, 34
Beowulf, 28, 29, 38, 49, 95, 119,
    121, 123

Beowulf, 5, 7, 78, 134
Beregond, 46
Beren, 82, 88
Bilbo, 8, 9–25, 29, 46, 58, 62, 69–70,
    85, 94, 121, 123
    as average, 38
    change in character of, 33–34,
        35–36
    as comfort-loving, 28
    development of, 93
    in the dragon's den, 37–38
    escape of, 22–23, 24, 32–33
    and the goblins, 23–24
    journey of, as metaphor, 30,
        38
    leap in the dark, 20–21
    maturity of, 30, 36
    quest of, 27
    rebirth of, 32, 33–34, 36
    and the Ring, 23–24, 32, 33, 45,
        56, 59, 80
    self-knowledge, 39
    and the spider, 34-36
    tension within, 30–31, 34
bird archetype, 34
Black Riders, 57
Bombadil, Tom, 6, 41, 43, 45, 48,
    58, 72–73, 83, 101–02, 103,
    118, 128
    as blind force, 149
    as eldest, 59, 60, 101–02
    power of, 148–49
    and the Ring, 56, 59
Boromir, 43, 45, 48, 57, 70, 97
    and the Ring, 61, 97
Bree, 43
Briareus, 119
Browning, Robert
    Childe Roland, 125
Butterbur, 70

Cacambo, 124
Cain (Biblical), 128
Campbell, Joseph, 117
Candide, 124
Celeborn, 45
Celebrimbor, 82
Chanson de Roland, 3
Charybdis, 120
Chaucer, Geoffrey
    Pardoner's Tale, 116
Chesterton, G.K., 6
Christ, 72, 73, 121, 123
Christensen, Bonniejean, 3, 78
Circe, 120
circle, as Jungian archetype, 32
Clytemnestra, 106
Cirith Ungol, 130, 131
city, symbolism of, 128
communism, 108-09

Déagol, 48
Denethor, 43, 47, 57, 61, 62, 70, 80,
    127
    death of, 130
    and the Ring, 62
the Deep, 146, 147
Dernhelm, 127
desire, complexity of, 141
Devouring Mother archetype, 32, 34
Donne, John, 5, 115
Durin, 82
dragon, symbolism of, 134

Eärendil, 82
earth navel, 115-16, 128
Eddas, 5
Elbereth, 103
Elendil, 82
Eliot, T.S.
    Waste Land, 125
Ellwood, Gracia Fay
    Good News from Middle Earth, 1
Elrond, 36, 45, 46-47, 57, 61, 86, 97,
    100
entrelacement, 4
Éomer, 49, 70, 127

Éowyn, 64, 70, 127
Eurydice, 28
Eve (Biblical), 47

The Faerie Queen. See Spenser: *The*
    Faerie Queen
fairy tales, hazardous morality of,
    50-51
Fangorn, 56, 58
Faramir, 47, 57, 61, 62, 70, 82
    rescue of, 130
    and the Ring, 62, 86
Farmer Cotton, 108, 109, 110
Farmer Giles of Ham, 78
Farmer Maggot, 117
fascism, 108-09, 110
Fatty Bolger, 100
Faulkner, William, 78
Ferny, Bill, 70
"fey," 127
Fitzgerald, Edward, 141
folk tales, psychoanalytic reading of,
    28-29
Freud, Sigmund, 28, 29
Frodo, 45, 46, 56, 57, 58, 69-70,
    79-80, 82-84, 87-88, 94, 95,
    98, 100-03, 106, 111, 117
    and the Barrow-wight, 118
    dreams of, 83-84
    as fey, 127
    as heroic, 57, 62
    journey to hell, 124-25
    rescue of, 126
    and the Ring, 59, 60, 61, 62-63,
        81, 86, 96-97, 101, 122
    and self-knowledge, 121-22
    and Shelob, 82, 131
Frye, Northrop, 69
Fuller, Edmund, 2, 41

Galadriel, 57, 60, 82, 94, 100, 135
Gamgee, Sam. *See* Sam
Gandalf, 45, 46-47, 62, 64, 80, 84,
    100, 103, 119, 121, 130
    and the Balrog, 43, 46, 122-23
    on Bombadil, 149

death of, 124
in *The Hobbit*, 30, 31, 33, 34, 39
and the Ring, 49, 57, 59, 60, 86, 96, 135
as White Rider, 48
Garden of Eden, 141
mist in, 145
Gawain, 39, 118
Gawain, 5
Genesis (Biblical), 128, 149
George, St., 38
Gildor, 86
Gil-galed, 82
Gimli, 46, 56, 84, 122, 133
Glamdring the Foe-Hammer, 29
Glorfindel, 149
goblins, as orcs, 67
Goldberry, 41, 46, 83, 86, 101, 102
Gollum, 29, 32, 45, 46, 48, 49, 56, 63, 80, 82, 96, 97, 123, 124–25
changes in character of, 7–8, 10–11, 12, 15, 17–18, 24
as evil, 7-8
as Frodo's alter ego, 122
grace in, 8
in *The Hobbit*, 7–8, 9–25
in *The Lord of the Rings*, 7–8, 12
and promise-keeping, 10–11, 147–48
and the Ring, 12, 58, 81, 86
split character of, 58
Gondor, 42
Grahame, Kenneth
Wind in the Willows, 28
Grass, Günter, 78
Grendel, 7, 28, 29
Grima, 70
Gwaihir, 84, 85, 97

Haggard, Rider, 6
'Hansel and Gretel', 51
Havelock the Dane, 41
Hawthorne, Nathaniel, 49
Heinlein, Robert
Stranger in a Strange Land, 106
Heracles, 121

Heraclitus, 120
Herbert, Frank
Dune, 106
Hesse, Hermann
Steppenwolf, 106
Hill, Helen, 4
Hitler, Adolf, 109
The Hobbit. See Tolkien: *The Hobbit*
hobbits
characteristics of, 68–69
as Everyclod, 69, 70, 71
as "normal people," 67
Hodgart, Matthews, 3
Homer, 116
Odyssey, 106
Hurd, Bishop, 75
Huttar, Charles A., 5

individuation process, 30
interlace technique, in literature, 76–77
as open-ended, 87
Isengard, 44, 80, 133
Isildur, 64, 81, 102

'Jack the Giant Killer', 50
Jason, 119
'The Jew among Thorns', 51, 52
Job (Biblical), 148
John, St., 145
journey to hell, mythological, 117, 121
Joyce, James, 78, 117
Jung, C.G., 28, 29, 30, 32, 34

Kaufmann, Milo, 6
Khayyam, Omar. *See* Omar Khayyam

Landroval, 85
Legolas, 47, 56, 84, 122, 133
Leviathan (Biblical), 148
Lewis, C.S., 2, 3, 4, 68, 70, 77
Screwtape Letters, 131

The Lord of the Rings. See Tolkien: *The Lord of the Rings*
Lot, Ferdinand, 76
Lucifer, 124
Lúthien Tinúviel, 82

MacCaffrey, Isabel C., 42
Mankato Studies in English, 1, 2, 5
Marlowe, 81
Matteotti, Giacomo, 110
Matthews, Dorothy, 3
medieval interlace, 75–76, 77, 81
Melchizedek (Biblical), 149
Meneldil, 47
Meneldor, 85
Meriadoc, 130
Merlin, 31, 80, 103
Merry, 44, 56, 57, 62, 64, 69, 79–80, 81, 97, 102, 117
    dream of, 85
Middle-earth, 116
    evil as more powerful in, 48–49
    "fairy" in, 68
    as morally charged, 42
    self-containment of, 52
Miller, David, 4, 69
Milton, John, 81, 135
    Paradise Lost, 49, 134
Minas Morgul, 130
Minas Tirith, 129-130
mining, satanic associations of, 134
Minotaur, 123
mithril, 134, 136
Moby-Dick, 41
modern novel, 78
Moorman, Charles, 49
Mordor, 42, 43, 46, 49, 82, 84, 87, 124–25, 131–32
    destruction of, 48, 85
    as hellish landscape, 124–25
Mordred, 28
Morgoth, 135
Moria, 122
Mussolini, Benito, 109–110
Mythlore, 1, 2
Mythopoeic Society, 1

Narsil, 72
Nazgûl, 57
Niggle, 142
    tree of, 143-44
    trip of, 143
Noah (Biblical), 128
Numenoreans, 43, 47

Odin, 31
Odysseus, 119, 120
Omar Khayyam, 141
Orcrist, 1, 2, 4, 5
Orcrist, the sword, 21, 29
orcs, 21
    as goblins, 67
    language of, 44
organic unity, in literature, 76, 78
Orpheus, 28, 121
Orthanc, 43
Ovid
    Metamorphoses, 77

paradise, 141–42
    and Abyss, 142, 145
Parish, 142, 144
Perkins, Agnes, 4
Pimple, 109
Pippin, 44, 46, 47, 49, 56, 62, 69, 79–80, 81, 84, 97, 121
    dream of, 85
Plank, Robert, 5
"precious bane," 135
'The Princess and the Pea', 51
Prometheus, 135
Prose Lancelot, 76
Proserpina, 116
Proust, Marcel, 78

Queste del Saint Graal, 77
Quickbeam, 41

Ready, William, 6
the Ring
    as corrupting, 56

destruction of, 126
as evil, 20, 23
in *The Hobbit*, 12–18, 20
power of, 56, 122
Ringwraiths, 56, 57
Rivendell, 118
Rogers, Deborah, 4, 6
Rosie, 106
'Rumpelstiltskin', 51

Sackville-Baggins, Lotho, 109
Sam, 45, 48, 58, 61, 69–70, 79–80,
    82–83, 87–88, 94, 97, 100,
    106, 118, 122, 125–26
as heroic, 57, 62, 70, 82
rescue of, 126
and the Ring, 59, 62-64
Sandyman, Ted, 45, 71
Saruman, 5, 43, 44, 59, 67, 71,
    80–81, 84, 109, 111, 132, 133
corruption of, 60
death of, 103, 107
and knowledge, 42, 45
and the Ring, 57, 60, 80
Sauron, 58, 60, 62, 80–81, 82, 87,
    95, 96, 97, 100, 102, 103, 109,
    122, 126, 131, 132
as evil, 13, 57, 135
and knowledge, 42, 45
and the Ring, 47, 49, 56, 57, 61,
    79, 132, 148
Scheps, Walter, 3
'The Scouring of the Shire', 105–06
as realistic, 106–07
Scylla, 120
Sharkey, 5, 100
Shelob, 48, 56, 59, 60, 82, 95, 127,
    131
the Shire, 43
changes in, 107–108, 112
fascism in, 108, 110–11
as caricature, 111
conquering of, 111
Smaug, 29, 36, 38, 42, 95
Smèagol, 58
Snowmane, 57
Sparks, Patricia Meyer, 42

Spenser, Edmund, 75, 77, 144
The Faerie Queen, 5, 49, 77
Strider, 43, 46, 64, 71, 100

technology, infernal side of, 135
Théoden, 45, 47, 57, 70, 80, 127
Theseus, 123
Thomson, George H., 75, 78, 79
Thorin, 39
Tolkien, J.R.R.
on allegory, 52, 55
and Catholic doctrine, 4
as Christian, 72
Chronology, 124
criticism of, 3–4
and fascism, 112
The Fellowship of the Ring, 5
The Frog King, 147
The Hobbit, 3, 56, 58, 67, 85, 93,
    123, 134
on evil, 7
folk ingredients of, 27–28
as foreshadowing *The Lord of
    the Rings*, 9, 11, 21, 23, 27
hobbits in, 68
as medieval, 78
quest in, 27
revisions of, 7–25
riddle contest in, 9–10, 48
and the Ring, changes in, 8,
    12-18, 20
hobbits in, 70
humans in, 70
'Leaf by Niggle', 6, 142–45
as allegory, 143
paradise in, 144–45
The Lord of the Rings, 2, 3–4, 5,
    6, 9, 21, 27, 106
as creation myth, 94
digression in, 101
dreams and nightmares in,
    83–86
dwarves in, 133
eagle motif in, 84-85
evil in, 7–8, 45
defeating of, 49
as more powerful, 49

recoiling on itself, 81, 82
as fairy tale, 50
fate/free will in, 100
forward to, 52, 111
good and evil in, 42–44,
  47–48, 135-36
grace in, 8
hell images/symbolism in,
  119–120, 130–33
hierarchy in, 47
hobbits in, 68
  initiation of, 121
human independence in,
  94
industrial/pastoral contrast in,
  133
instinct in, 45–46
interlace structure of, 75–76,
  81, 83, 86, 87
knowledge in, as corrupting,
  45
layers of time in, 101–03
light/dark archetypes in, 82
mapping the journey in,
  95–98
as medieval, 75, 78
moral absolutes in, 50
narrative texture of, 95
nine cycles of danger and
  rescue, 98–101
overall structure of, 79
places and colors in, 42–43
poems in, 78
power in, 47, 55
puns in, 46
purpose behind chance
events in, 86–87
quest in, 79–80, 94–95
  reversal of, 94–95
races in, 67–68
the road in, 93
as self-contained world,
  41–42, 52
shadow image in, 87
symbolic landscape of,
  128–29, 131
tragedy in, 98

unified structure of, 94
verbal taboo in, 46
war in, 80
on *The Lord of the Rings*,
  structure of, 79
medieval studies of, 78
and moral absolutism, 3–4
moral vision of, 135–36
myths in, 5
'On Fairy Stories', 146–47
paradise in, 6, 142, 144–45, 147
on power, 65
and promise-keeping, 147
as royalist, 64
'Scouring of the Shire', 105–06
  as realistic, 106–07
on 'Scouring of the Shire',
  111–12
on subcreation, 145
theism of, 149
transformation of ordinary in,
  146
The Two Towers, 129
Tolkien and the Critics, 1, 2
*Tolkien Criticism: An Annotated
  Checklist*, 1
Tolkien Journal, 1, 2
Took, Belladonna, 30
Tower of Babel, 128
Treebeard, 43, 44, 59, 60, 80

Ulysses, 106, 116
unconscious, and dreams, 28
underworld, 116
Unferth, 7

Vinaver, Eugène, 76
Vonnegut, Kurt
  Cat's Cradle, 106

West, Richard, 4
Wilson, Edmund, 2
Wordsworth, William, 149